WINDSURFING

Peter Hart

The Crowood Press

WINDSURFING

First published in 2004 by
The Crowood Press Ltd
Ramsbury, Marlborough
Wiltshire SN8 2HR

www.crowood.com

British Library Cataloguing-in-Publication Data
A catalogue record for this book is available from the British Library.

ISBN 1 86126 677 4

Dedication
To the memory of my father, a man of the sea, and to my mother, who bravely put up with the obsession.

Acknowledgements
The author would like to thank Annette Hart for her skill on the water and her patience at home; David White and John Carter for their efforts in the searing heat; and Tushingham Sails and Starboard boards for their continuous support.

Principal photographers: John Carter and David White

Disclaimer
Windsurfing is a potentially hazardous sport. The author and publisher disclaim any liability incurred in connection with the use of this data or specific details.

Typeset by Carreg Limited, Ross-on-Wye, Herefordshire

Printed and bound in Singapore by Craft Print International

CONTENTS

CHAPTER 1

INTRODUCTION

ABOUT WINDSURFING

Windsurfing. The name sums it up so well. You may never have surfed a wave but you can surely imagine the exhilaration of skimming over the water on a tiny craft, driven along by a clean, noiseless energy. Just replace the wave with a sail and some wind and you will come close to understanding the thrill, freedom and accessibility of windsurfing.

This sport of ours has come a long way since its crude beginnings in California in the late sixties, when the pioneers played around with what was little more than a Malibu surfboard and a colourful bag. Since then it has become an Olympic sport. Windsurfers have crossed the Atlantic and Pacific oceans. They have held the record for the fastest wind-powered craft, having clocked speeds of 80kph (50mph). Windsurfers jump, fly and ride 12m (40ft) waves. The top performers follow a professional world circuit where they compete over a variety of disciplines such as racing, freestyle and wave sailing. However, the windsurfer is also a very versatile craft, equally at home on the gentle waters of an inland lake and in the towering surf off Hawaii. And as a result, despite its 'whizzy' image, people of all ages and abilities enjoy windsurfing.

And is it difficult to learn? If, without any guidance, you take out an old board in a choppy sea on a windy day, it can be close to impossible. But, as the following pages will show, given some light, modern equipment, a gentle breeze, flat water and a game plan, almost anybody can learn to sail, turn round and come back within a few hours.

But to stop there would be like watching the adverts and then leaving as the credits roll for the main feature. It is the relentless mental and physical challenges of moving into stronger winds on higher performance gear and trying the endless moves, which leaves millions of people eternally gripped by windsurfing.

A PATH TO THE TOP

Here is your route to windsurfing mastery.

Step 1 – Up and Back

Your career starts in a light wind, on a large, stable board with a small and very light sail. In this first session you are bombarded with new sensations. You re figuring out how the wind works, how the sail drives the board at the same time trying to keep your footing on a sensitive platform AND control the pull in the sail. Yes at first there is a touch of slapping your head and rubbing your tummy with different hands syndrome but it all falls into place very quickly. The key aims are to learn how to raise the rig, turn the board round on the spot and take up a comfortable sailing position. To become the complete master of your destiny, you then learn how to steer and how to adjust body and rig for the various sailing courses.

The first session is about taking on the very basics of balance and board control. (John Carter)

You can experience the joys of planing within weeks of learning. (John Carter)

A larger sail forces you to lean out against the rig. (John Carter)

Step 2 – More Power, More Speed

Soon you realise that this is a Formula I car and you're using it do the shopping. The next step is to tap into more power either by using a bigger sail or waiting for more wind.

Suddenly the stakes are raised. You have to hang right away from the boom and use your body as a counter-weight. More power in the sail translates immediately into more speed, faster manoeuvring and the need for more precise technique.

Step 3 – The Harness, Footstraps and Planing

This is no longer a gentle mode of transport, it's a sport and your already over-worked arms are the first to feel it. Now is the time to attach the harness. The harness is a light, padded belt with a hook on the front, which fastens around your waist. Two lines form a loop on either side of the boom. When you drop the hook onto the line, you can then use your body-weight to take the lion's share of the force,

leaving the arms free to make the minor adjustments.

The premier goal is to learn to handle enough power to make the board plane. Planing – it's what ALL windsurfers are fundamentally designed to do. Like a speed boat, when they reach a certain speed, they rise out of the water and skim along the surface. Your speed immediately doubles as does the thrill. The larger modern boards plane in relatively little wind so you can attain this Holy Grail of planing within a few weeks of learning.

With planing speed, you need an extra degree of control. Footstraps – loops on the deck that you slide you feet under – give you that control.

With your feet in the straps, you can hold a secure stance in the rough, keep your footing as water sweeps across the board and, ultimately, control the board in the air. You can fit and practise with the footstraps in light winds and at slow speeds. The idea is to get used to sailing and balancing with the feet locked in one position before doing the same in planing conditions.

Step 4 – Waterstarts, Smaller Boards, Carving Turns

As soon as your sail control in stronger winds is more or less instinctive, you learn the waterstart, a technique where you allow the rig to pull you out of the water and onto the board. It's a life changing skill which not only allows you to start off effortlessly in strong winds but which also allows you to experiment on smaller boards.

Able to waterstart and plane hooked in the harness and with the feet in the straps, your board is no longer a dinghy without a seat, it's a surfboard and needs to be handled as such. Steering from now on comes less from moving the rig and more from simple foot pressure. You want to turn left? Then pressure the left hand edge, bank the board over and feel it carve around like a surfboard or a waterski.

The carve gybe, an 180 degree downwind turn, is windsurfing's blue riband move. Considerable forces build up if you throw any vehicle into a turn at 20 mph plus and you have to take up some dynamic postures to withstand those forces.

A small board carves through the turns like a water-ski. (Dave White)

Step 5 – Endless Avenues

Where you go from here depends on the level of your ambition and the conditions available to you. Waves, flat water, racing, trick sailing and gentle cruising all beckon if you have the time to practise and the right equipment.

HOW TO START

The easiest, safest and most effective road into the sport is through an official RYA (Royal Yachting Association) course. At centres that carry the flag, you can be con-fident that the equipment, instructors, sail-ing area, general facilities and rescue craft are all in place and up to scratch. The scheme itself is clear and logical – but that is the sort of appraisal you're bound to hear from someone who has had a hand in developing it!

But it is certainly not the only way. Many people get into the sport through people they know, and friends often make good teachers because they are bursting with enthusiasm. You just need to be pos-itive that your chosen friend is of sound mind and body and not the type who would send a non-swimmer out on to a churning ocean in an offshore wind.

The good thing about the RYA scheme is that there are specialist courses or 'clin-ics' for every level on every aspect of the sport. You can, therefore, dip in and out at any time to have either a technical makeover or to learn a completely new set of skills and manoeuvres.

There are recognized centres all over the world. Contact the RYA (see page 174) to find the one nearest to you.

With the basic skills under your belt, the sky is literally the limit. (John Carter)

CHAPTER 2

EQUIPMENT

Close your ears, at all costs, to the following advice: 'it doesn't matter what equipment you choose because, as a beginner, you won't be good enough to tell the difference'. Having the right gear is as important for the beginner as it is for the seasoned pro. If windsurfing has a reputation for being difficult to learn, this is entirely down to people being put on heavy old equipment of the wrong size and wrong design – sometimes by well-meaning friends, sometimes by less than reputable hire centres.

GETTING STARTED

At first, all you need is to be handed the right equipment and be allowed to get on with it. An advantage of learning at a recognized school is that you will be provided with a suitable board and rig that is set up for your height and weight, leaving you free to concentrate on balance and reacting to the force in the sail. If a friend is teaching you, be sure that the sail is no bigger than 5sq m.

Equipment makes more sense and becomes much more interesting once you've had a go. Find out how it all fits together, both to give you a degree of independence from the outset and so you can de-rig the sail on the water, stow it away and paddle home if the wind drops or you have some kind of problem.

Very soon after these first steps you will need to develop a deeper understanding of the equipment if you wish to continue to improve. Although boards and rigs are incredibly versatile and capable of operating in a variety of wind and sea conditions, they do have their limitations and the more exciting aspects of the sport are only open to you if you have the right equipment. You must be able to recognize when your current combination is holding you back and the time has come to trade up. However, more important than gathering a quiver of different boards and sails for every conceivable eventuality, is an understanding of how to customize and tune the equipment for your specific needs. Footstrap placement, rig tension, harness line position, boom height, choice of fin and sail size all exert a huge influence

This photo of an entry-level model shows the footstraps, the mast-track, the slot for the daggerboard and the mast base. The board has a shock absorbing, soft rubber deck. Most boards, however, are simply covered in textured, non-slip paint. (John Carter)

The two light wind options:
(above) a retracting daggerboard;
(below) a removable central fin. (John Carter)

The boom clamp fits around the mast, holding it tightly between a set of padded jaws. It is tensioned and released by a lever.

The sail is made of strong, light, stable and mostly see-through film.

Battens are stiffening strips of fibreglass or carbon that run horizontally across the sail to help stabilize its shape.

The mast tapers gradually towards the top and supports the front edge of the sail.

The boom is the wishbone-shaped appliance you hang on to in order to control the rig.

The uphaul is the thick, sometimes elasticated, rope attached to the front end of the boom, which you use to pull the rig out of the water.

The outhaul rope runs through a pulley system in the end of the boom and secures the outer end of the sail to the boom.

The mastfoot/extension slides up the mast and connects the rig to the mast base.

The downhaul rope attaches the bottom of the sail to the mastfoot and is tensioned via series of pulleys.

The mast-track, a recess that accommodates the mastfoot, is on the top of the board just forward of the daggerboard. Most mast-tracks allow for about 20cm (8in) of adjustment forward or back to allow you to trim the board for different sail sizes and wind strengths.

The fin fits to the underside of the tail of the board. In light winds it lends directional stability. In strong winds, the size and design of the fin has a massive influence on how early the board planes and its handling at speed and around the turns.

The deck is the top of the board.

Footstraps anchor your feet to the board and lend extra control at speed. The wide choice of screw holes allows you to set them up in a number of positions, according to your size and standard. Footstraps will not be fitted for your first session.

The daggerboard or central fin makes the board more stable at rest and gives it a pivot point to turn around in light winds. Its use is mostly restricted to light winds or for learning. With a push of the foot, it retracts right up into the hull. Some models feature a central, removable fin instead.

The universal joint is the rubber joint at the bottom of the mastfoot that allows the rig to fall in any direction.

The mast base screws into the mast-track and accommodates mastfoot/extension by use of a locking pin.

The Board and Rig (John Carter)

Boards for all seasons. From left to right: a Formula racing board; a de-tuned version for learning and improving in light to moderate winds; a 130ltr free-ride board for planing winds; a specialized freestyle model; and, on the far right, an 83ltr wave board. (John Carter)

The wider the board and the bigger the sail, the more fin area you need to resist it. The three more upright shapes on the left offer a good compromise between power and easy turning. The two short, wide, swept-back designs on the right offer extreme manoeuvrability for freestyle and wave sailing.

Volume in action – 200 versus 100ltr. No prizes for guessing which is better for light winds!
(John Carter)

on your comfort and how well the board performs in different situations.

BOARDS – SIZES AND DESIGNS

Boards come in a bewildering variety of shapes, so volume, measured in litres, is the easiest dimension to relate to early on. The bigger the board, the bigger the sail it is designed to carry and the lighter the wind it is designed to be used in. Under the feet of an average adult weighing 75kg (165lb), any board with 170ltr of volume or more provides a stable platform for sailing in light wind. It is easy to sail and manoeuvre off the plane and therefore good for learning.

However, it is not a case of big boards being good for beginners and little boards

being suitable for experts. The highest specification racing boards have upwards of 200ltr of volume. They need the buoyancy primarily to support the weight of a huge sail, which produces the power to get them scorching along in relatively light winds.

As you move down towards the 130ltr mark, the board will still support the weight of the sailor and rig when stationary but it is fundamentally designed for stronger winds and planing and therefore a higher skill level is required. In most instances it is too unstable for learning in light winds.

Boards below about 100ltr need to be moving before they will fully support the weight of the sailor (again, assuming a weight of around 75kg/165lb) and rig. An experienced windsurfer may have the skill

and balance to climb on and pull the rig up in the conventional fashion, but he will be partially under water. From this stage on, the waterstart is the essential starting method.

As to which size of board is easiest to sail, it depends on the strength of the wind and the standard of the sailor. In light to moderate winds, beginners and intermediates will favour bigger boards due to their inherent stability. As the wind gets up, however, big boards become increasingly difficult to control. They bounce along the surface, the waves knock them off course and they present too much area to the wind, which can get under the hull and literally blow them out of the water. A smaller board, in the same conditions, stays in contact with the water and can be kept on course with the slightest heel or toe pressure, so long as it is under the control of a skilled pilot.

Volume only determines the wind range the board is to be used in and the weight and standard of the sailor it is designed for. The other design elements such as length, width and curve decide where its performance strengths lie.

Width and Length

Boards vary relatively little in length these days. With only a few exceptions, they are no longer than 2.8m with the shortest being around 2.2m. It is in the width of the board that the major differences lie. The big light-wind boards measure up to a metre at their widest point. The smallest high-wind board will be less than half that.

Building the extra volume into the width has been found to be far more effective than extending the length. A shorter, wider board is easier to control, more manoeuvrable both in rough seas and on flat water, and earlier to plane than a long thin board of the same volume.

Width in different sections of the board also makes a big difference to performance. A wide tail, for example, is good for early planing and tight radius turns but will make the board less controllable at high speeds. A narrow tail increases your control at high speeds and through long fast turns but is not so good for acceleration.

Other Features

Some more board design features you should become familiar with include:

*   The rocker line. This describes the curve of the board as viewed from the side.
*   The plan shape. The outline of the board as viewed from above.
*   The rails. The edges of the board.

It is difficult to consider these features in isolation, as it is how they all combine that determines the board's performance and suitability for different conditions and sailing styles.

In general, straight lines and sharp edges translate into speed. Curves translate into manoeuvrability. So it is that both light and strong wind racing boards, whose chief weapon is speed, have parallel sides, a straight, flat underneath shape and sharp edges. All of these design features ensure that they skim smoothly over the water and meet with minimum resistance. To a certain degree, however, those same features hinder manoeuvrability and force the sailor into making long, safe turns.

At the other end of the scale, the wave board is curved in every dimension. The water sucks in around those curves creating more drag (less speed) but it also means you can bank the board over like a surfboard and it will follow the contour of those curves to make super-tight carving turns.

BOARDS – CATEGORIES

It is useful to understand the various board categories just to help you grasp what is being talked about in brochures, magazines and test reports.

There are two major categories: specialist boards, designed to excel in the competitive disciplines of racing, wave sailing, freestyle and speed sailing; and 'all-round' recreational boards, designed to do a bit of everything.

The straight lines of the racing board and the curves and rounded rails of the wave board represent the two extremes of the design spectrum. (John Carter)

Racing Boards

Windsurfing has a variety of racing disciplines with models for each.

The Olympic Board

In the Olympics, competitors all use the same model, which is selected some years before the games. Since the Barcelona games in 1992, the chosen board has been the Mistral One design. This traditional board is 3.8m long with a central daggerboard. Although wildly out of date as a design, it is still favoured by the authorities as it can be raced in the very light winds that often prevail at the Olympic venues.

Formula Boards

Almost as wide as they are long, Formula boards have taken competitive windsurfing into new areas both in terms of looks and performance. The revolutionary design includes a massive fin and sail, enabling the board to plane in winds of just 7–10kt (force 3). The racers compete around a long, square course so the board has to perform on all points of sailing – 'upwind' (towards), 'downwind' (away from) and across the wind – and it does so incredibly efficiently, often travelling at twice the speed of the wind.

On the downside, they are very expensive and, being a development class, they are soon superseded by something just a little bit better and so have little residual value. Despite being designed for winds under 20kn, the extreme positioning of the footstraps combined with the fearsome power of the sail and fin, make them a real challenge to sail.

Formula boards range in size from about 180–200ltr.

Slalom Boards

These are basically speed machines. Slalom, windsurfing's re-emerging discipline, involves shorter races, mostly across the wind, with a number of gybe buoys (marks where you have to turn). The boards not only have to be fast but also

The UK's Dom Tidy powering upwind on the traditionally shaped Olympic board. He is standing right out on the rail to balance the lift from the daggerboard. (Barrie Edgington)

manoeuvrable. The moderate wind models look like mini-Formula boards. On or off the racetrack, they are a lot of fun.

Slalom boards range in size from about 75–130ltr.

Wave Boards

Wave boards are fundamentally surfboards with a sail. The accent is heavily on manoeuvrability in the most extreme situations, like in the air and on the face of a wave. However, they are slower in a straight line and slower to accelerate and to plane than a more all-round design. The smaller wave boards offer the best control in high winds in or out of the waves.

Wave boards range in size from about 60–100ltr.

Freestyle Boards

The wave of weird and wonderful 'new-school', skateboard-style tricks has spawned a breed of board that is very quick to plane, turns on a sixpence, jumps with the slightest encouragement and has channels in the nose and tail to allow it to slide forwards, backwards and every which way. They are also relatively wide and stable enough to allow the trickster to recover from extreme angles. They sound like the ideal machine for improver and expert alike. But the one thing they are not so good at is blasting along in a straight line at speed in choppy water, and that is what the majority of people want to do.

Freestyle boards range in size from about 90–120ltr.

Free-Wave or Free-Move Boards

Part freestyle, part wave board, this hybrid is aimed at those who want to take their freestyle routines into small waves. They have the basic outline and nose 'kick' of a wave board to allow them to manoeuvre on waves and handle steep landings, but a straighter rocker line to give them more speed and acceleration.

Free-wave boards range in size from about 75–90ltr.

Long and thin became short and fat and the process of balancing and learning became infinitely easier. The traditional shape on the right is actually quite wide compared to the original windsurfer. (John Carter)

Free-Ride Boards

The 'free-ride' label was borrowed from snowboarding in the early nineties. Basically, it described the act of sliding around the mountain and then dealing with whatever you came across, be it groomed *piste*, powder snow, slush, bumps, drop-offs or natural jumps. Consequently, a very versatile snowboard was needed.

This is equally true in windsurfing – the free-ride board is designed to do a bit of everything in a wide range of conditions. The recreational windsurfer wants to go fast but also wants to enjoy the turns. One day he may be going for top speed on flat water; the next, the wind may have changed strength and direction and he finds himself in breaking surf trying to ride and jump small waves.

Free-ride is actually a pretty nebulous category encompassing all manner of boards. The biggest are de-tuned Formula boards. Although easier to sail, they are still designed to support a huge rig and get going in very light winds. Below that, the size indicates the intended use – the smaller the board, the higher the wind strength it is designed to perform in and the smaller the ideal sail size.

Free-ride boards range in size from about 80–200ltr.

Entry-Level Boards

People entering or returning to the sport are often surprised by the sight of the entry-level windsurfer. Most people expect a long and thin replica of the original Malibu surfboard but what stands in front of them is more like a door. What was once long and thin is now short and wide.

Although the traditional shapes still exist, the schools that continue to teach on them are few and far between. There are many advantages to the new shape but

the main one is stability, the beginner's ultimate companion. Stability at slow speeds comes from width not length, so it is that the wide boards are very hard to fall off. There is really no such thing as a dedicated beginner's board on the market these days. The short, wide design favoured by many beginners is virtually identical to the highest performance racing boards. The only differences are:

- The entry-level version will be of heavier but more durable and of impact-resistant construction.
- It may have a soft rubber deck – a generally more friendly surface that absorbs the unsubtle scramblings of the beginner. It also offers a good grip – a slippery surface underfoot makes it impossible for you to relax and balance. It will have either a removable central fin or a daggerboard for stability in light winds.
- It will have a vast choice of potential footstrap positions. Some are located far forward, just behind the mast base, so you can get used to using the footstraps off the plane in light winds.

The huge advantage of learning on such a board is that it is wide enough to support a novice sailing in light winds, but it also has the design pedigree to accelerate smoothly on to the plane as the power increases, providing an easy and gradual introduction to higher performance windsurfing.

THE RIG

The rig, which comprises the mast, sail boom and mastfoot is effectively your motor. The amount of power produced is proportional to the strength of the wind and the size of the sail.

Little more than a colourful bag twenty years ago, the rig is now a highly precise aerofoil, constructed out of a mixture of sailcloth and exotic, non-stretch, see-through film. It is an extraordinary bit of kit. The fact that in breaking surf, it can be pummelled by literally hundreds of tons of foaming water and surface without a scratch, says enough.

It acts much like a wing, in that wind accelerates faster over one side to create a pressure differential, which in turn generates the lift to drive the board along. (Actually the board is sucked along but let us not disappear into the jungle of aerodynamics.)

Equally beneficial to the sailor is the rig's ability to twist, flex and literally shape itself to the wind, and deal with the small changes in strength and direction – so long as it is properly tensioned.

Sails – Sizes, Designs and Categories

The most influential factors in sail design are the size of the sail and the wind strength it needs to be able to withstand.

For adults, sails range in size from about 3–12sq m. The largest are hugely powerful racing sails. The smallest are either for use in very high winds or for beginners looking

for an easy time. The commonest sail sizes used by proficient adult recreational sailors who want enough power to plane in moderate to fresh winds are about 4–8.5sq m.

Just as with boards, there is a range of designs to suit the various sailing disciplines. And also like boards, it is important to strike the right balance between the mutually exclusive qualities of speed/power and manoeuvrability. For example, a sail with a full shape will have a lot of pull and drive but will be heavy to throw around. A sail with a flatter profile will generally be lighter and easier to handle during manoeuvres but will be short on raw power.

Race Sails
These are hugely powerful, designed to handle a lot of wind and place the racer right on the edge of control. The wider luff

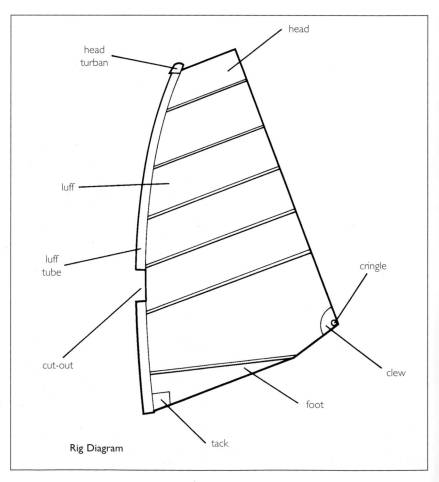

Rig Diagram

tube accommodates 'camber inducers', tuning fork-shaped widgets that connect the batten to the mast and stabilize the front of the sail.

Wave Sails
Built to withstand the unholy forces exerted by breaking surf, wave sails have a flatter profile and so sacrifice some raw power in favour of manoeuvrability.

Freestyle Sails
Essentially very light in the hands and easy to throw around, freestyle sails provide good acceleration but often not the best top speed.

Free-Ride Sails
Free-ride sails make up about 90 per cent of all sails sold. Designed to work in a wide range of conditions, they are easy to rig and probably offer the best compromise between speed and ease of handling.

Masts
The mast is crucial to how the sail sets. Each sail is designed to take a mast of a certain length and stiffness. The stiffness is measured on the IMCS (International Mast Check System) scale, which measures how much the mast flexes under load. The scale ranges from 19 (soft) to 30 (stiff). Details of the appropriate mast are actually printed on most sails.

Masts are usually made from a mixture of carbon and fibreglass. The higher the carbon content, the lighter and more responsive the sail feels. However, carbon is more fragile and more expensive.

Ever more popular are the narrower RDM (reduced diameter masts) or 'skinnies' as they are more popularly known. There is a continuing debate as to whether they improve the sail's performance but it is indisputable that, due to the extra thickness of the walls, they are appreciably stronger and so a natural choice for many wave sailors. Smaller people, or least those with small hands, find them easier to grab and hang on to in mid-manoeuvre.

Booms
Booms are made from high-grade aluminium or carbon. The latter is lighter and stiffer but more expensive. Unless it is to be used with a very big sail (7sq m plus), the benefits of a carbon boom are less marked as those of a carbon mast.

Booms have a telescopic back end, which usually extends about 40cm (16in) to fit a variety of sail sizes. To cover a reasonable sail range of about 4–7.5sq m, you can get away with just two booms.

Boom arms come in different diameters and the one you find the most comfortable will depend on the size of your hands, but many prefer the narrower gauge.

Starting Out
Nothing is guaranteed to sap both your energy and enthusiasm more quickly than repeatedly trying to heave up a heavy rig. This may be because the rig is too big but often it is down to certain schools using baggy, low-tec heaps of ancient junk. These days, a good school will use light monofilm sails and carbon masts – the difference is incomparable.

The instructor should assess your weight and the wind strength and relieve you of the burden of choosing a sail size. In the ideal learning conditions of a 3–6kt (force 2) wind (see page 26) an adult

Carbon masts make the rig lighter and more responsive. Some wave sailors favour the thinner diameter 'skinny' on the left because of its extra strength. (Dave White)

For ease of travel and storage, most masts break down into two pieces – and sometimes more if you abandon them in the waves! (Dave White)

For your safety and pleasure, you have to get the right size rig for your standard, the wind strength and what you want to do. A giant 12sq m sail is perfect for racing champion Ross Williams but a 2sq m sail is better for his six-year-old apprentice. (John Carter)

weighing 70kg (155lb) would be using a sail of about 4sq m. It is important that the sail generates a reasonable amount of power so you are forced to counterbalance that pull with your body weight and develop an effective posture…and get a damp rap on the knuckles if you don't. If the sail is too small or the wind too light, it's like holding a damp lettuce leaf. You get no feeling for the trim and balance and so quickly develop a multitude of bad habits.

OTHER GEAR

Windsurfing is a total immersion sport. Falling in is not a surprise or a shock; just part of the game, often the hilarious result of trying something new. Windsurfing has such an amazing safety record because we recognize that fact and dress for the water.

And please forget about the supposed cold. At most times of year, even in the UK, you will return from a session literally steaming thanks to the wonders of the modern wetsuit.

Wetsuits

First and foremost, a wetsuit has to keep you warm but it must also allow you to move with feline stealth and freedom. So it is that the modern wetsuit is basically an insulated, waterproof leotard.

A windsurfing wetsuit is made from either single- or double-lined neoprene rubber. Double-lined neoprene has a

nylon layer bonded to both sides of the rubber. The nylon limits the rubber's natural stretch but because it absorbs a little water it can lead to some wind chill – however, it is very durable and consequently the choice of most schools.

Single-lined neoprene, also known as 'smooth skin', has a shiny rubber finish like that of a seal. It is more flexible than double-lined neoprene and since the water runs straight off it, there is little or no wind chill. On the downside, it is more easily snagged and torn.

The thickness of the neoprene varies depending on the season it has been designed for. Winter suits are usually 4–5mm thick over the main part of the body. Suits for the summer and spring are

A snug-fitting, flexible, one-piece wetsuit with a little room around the forearms and shoulders is best for windsurfing. Despite the name, it should keep you as dry as possible. (John Carter)

Windsurfers at all levels of proficiency will sometimes end up fully immersed. A wetsuit not only has to keep you warm but must also allow you to move freely and swim. (John Carter)

typically 3mm thick and may also have short arms.

The wetsuit works by keeping the body dry and insulated. If water does penetrate, it is trapped and forms a thin layer between body and suit. It is then warmed by the body and provides extra insulation. For this to work, the suit must be tight fitting over the legs and main part of the body.

The fit is as important as thickness to the warmth of a wetsuit. If it is baggy or, worst of all, loose at the neck, cold water flushes through the suit every time you fall in. If it is too tight, it takes a concerted effort just to move and breathe.

A well-stocked shop may carry suits for many different water sports so make sure you are in the windsurfing section. A suit designed for windsurfing has a more generous cut around the upper back so that it is comfortable when your arms are up and stretched out forwards. The forearms will also be looser to give those hard-working muscles room to expand and prevent cramp.

Footwear

As well as providing warmth and grip, shoes or boots protect the sole against sharp objects on the seabed and the whole foot should it slip and cannon into the mast base.

Specialist shoes and boots have a neoprene upper that is stitched and glued to a soft rubber sole. Shoes must be tight fitting or they rip off when you fall in.

You can use an old pair of trainers for learning but the thicker, heavier and stiffer the sole, the less sensitive you are to what's going on, which is why a large proportion of experts elect to go barefoot.

Neoprene shoes for summer and boots for winter. (GUL International)

Gloves of any kind restrict your grip but this curved finger model helps you hang on to the boom. (GUL International)

Gloves

The modern boom has a soft, textured grip so gloves are not really necessary for your first sessions.

However, if you are susceptible to blistering or foresee a series of lengthy sailing periods – on holiday, for example – a pair of fingerless sailing gloves will go some way to prevent blistering. The problem is worse in hot climates where the warm water softens the hands.

Ultimately, the best protection against blistering is to windsurf as much as you can and develop horny calluses all over your palms.

Neoprene hats – very efficient without winning any fashion awards. (GUL International)

Gloves of any kind are not popular as they restrict your grip on the boom, force you to hold on tighter and make the forearms give out prematurely. Even in the depths of winter, many prefer to go without. However, those who do wear gloves tend to favour one of the following:

- Gloves with pre-shaped, curved fingers that help you grip the boom.
- Palmless gloves or mitts. This open style of glove where just the top is insulated offers the best grip although the skin is open to the elements.
- Washing-up gloves. Thin, cheap and useful for keeping the wind off.

Hats

A huge percentage of body heat escapes through the head so a neoprene hat can prolong your sailing time by hours as winter closes in. However, as hearing has an extraordinary effect on balance, make sure the ears remain open to the wind.

Helmets

The latest water sports hard hat is light, comfortable and looks business-like. However, whilst some elect to wear one, the majority do not. I can offer no logical explanation apart from the fact that head injuries are rare and that helmets have yet to be fully absorbed into windsurfing culture.

There is anecdotal evidence that helmets can give you an unreal sense of your own safety and make you take unwise risks. I wear one when going for a new move, where I am not sure of the outcome. Some aerial moves, notably loops,

Windsurfing helmets are light and stylish these days. 'Head injuries may be rare but you never know…' is the philosophy of wave sailor Corky Kirkham. (John Carter)

which fail to go according to plan, can end up with you being slammed to the water on the side of your face. A helmet goes a long way to protecting you from a burst eardrum.

A helmet will also protect you when windsurfing on crowded waters where there is a real risk of being hit by someone else's falling rig. But enough of such horror stories – as a first timer, the school may offer you a helmet but you will not be made to wear it.

Buoyancy Aids

The message on buoyancy aids is straightforward – if it makes you feel happier and more confident in the water, then wear it. There is no stigma attached.

On a beginner's course you will be asked to wear a buoyancy aid and they are also compulsory on certain inland waters that come under the jurisdiction of a local water authority. Otherwise, it is a matter of personal choice. The majority choose to go without.

In most situations, when you fall off, you surface right by your board, a huge buoyancy aid in itself. The wetsuit also has a certain amount of buoyancy. So you do not have to be a strong swimmer to enjoy windsurfing. In situations where you might lose the board – namely in breaking surf – a buoyancy aid can actually hinder you because it restricts your swimming action and prevents you ducking under the bigger waves.

However, a buoyancy aid can be useful for the more experienced windsurfer. In the waterstart, for example, it helps to float you in the start position and saves a huge amount of energy.

DRESS FOR THE OCCASION

I'm not afraid to admit this – I once entered the first stages of hypothermia whilst windsurfing in Barbados. I have also suffered from severe heat exhaustion and dehydration to the point where I could barely function whilst windsurfing in England.

In Barbados, I was enjoying a fantastic day in the waves, sailing just in a pair of shorts. After three hours, a rainsquall came

Windsurfing clad only in a kilt, in the North Atlantic in October, is not to be generally recommended, but this is what you expect from eccentric Irishman Timo Mullen. (John Carter)

through. The wind increased and the temperature dropped a little (by normal standards it was still baking). However, that combination of extreme physical effort, wind chill (the act of the wind literally whipping heat away from the skin) and a drop in temperature, was enough to make my body core temperature drop and for me to suddenly become disorientated and uncoordinated. Luckily I was close to shore.

In England, I had simply put the wrong wetsuit in the car. It was a summer's day and I was forced to wear a winter suit. Within half an hour I was teetering on the verge of collapse and barely had the energy to crawl back up the beach. The wetsuit was so efficient that the body had no way of cooling itself.

Dressing for windsurfing is about protecting yourself from the prevailing conditions. This may mean wearing a hat, a T-shirt and smearing yourself with factor 40 sun cream or wrapping every exposed square millimetre of skin in neoprene.

How you dress also depends on the sort of session you have in mind. For example, if you are planning an hour of general freestyle or intense manoeuvre practice in benign conditions on enclosed waters, you can dress fairly scantily. However, more clothing should be worn if you are off on a long coastal cruise where, in the event of a problem, you may have to spend a long time in the water.

As a general observation, I think that many people wear too much. I'm not suggesting doing anything that might lessen

your general water confidence and safety but there are those who load themselves up with so many accessories that they lumber around like the first moonwalker. Freedom of movement is a safety aid in itself.

RIGGING

The act of assembling the rig is childishly simple. Every modern rig package comes with a detailed set of instructions specific to that brand so there is no real excuse for getting it wrong. Problems come from a failure to grasp what a colossal influence rigging has on performance, especially in stronger winds; hence in their haste to get out there, people hurl it together believing that it doesn't really matter.

Slide the mast up the sleeve, pointed end first.

The mastfoot/extension fits into the base of the mast. The downhaul is then attached to the foot of the sail, in this case via a hook and pulley block. When it is tensioned, the hook will come down right to the base of the mast. The extension allows you to adjust the length of the mast to fit the sail exactly.

The jaws clamp around the boom and are locked in place by a lever.

The outhaul rope controls the fullness and power in the bottom of the sail. It threads through the eyelet in the clew and back into a cleat on the back of the boom. Tension it so the sail forms a smooth curve and the belly of the sail is not touching the boom. Adjust the length of the boom so that the clew pulls right to the end.

Rigging Sequence *(John Carter)*

able to soften the effects of gusts and lulls. Without that flexibility, you would feel every pressure change and would constantly have to adjust the sail angle to avoid being pulled off balance.

The amount of power the sail produces and the degree of twist and flexibility is controlled via the downhaul and outhaul ropes.

The Downhaul

By downhauling you put tension into the front of the sail, which is essential to its stability. It also compresses the mast and makes it bend. Being thinner, the top bends more and, as it does so, the head of the sail flattens off. Downhauling also makes the leech go loose, which allows the sail to flex and twist.

The greater the downhaul tension, within reason, the more stable the sail will be, the more it can twist and handle the gusts so the more suited it is for strong winds. Too much downhaul tension will cause the sail to rattle, shake and feel gutless. Under-tensioned, the power point of the sail wanders all over the place making it impossible for you to settle into a calm, controlled stance.

The commonest rigging ailment is too little downhaul, mainly because it can be very hard work, especially on big sails. Invest in a decent pulley system and keep the whole appliance free of sand and grit. If the rope bites into your hand, wrap it around a handle of some sorts. There are many downhauling tools but a harness hook does the job pretty well. If you are still struggling, collar someone large and muscular – it's a good way to meet people!

The Outhaul

The outhaul rope controls the fullness in the middle of the sail and therefore the power. You adjust it so there is a smooth curve in the sail. The symptoms of too much or too little tension are obvious. If the sail looks flat, has no shape through the middle, feels twitchy and provides little or no forward drive, there is too much outhaul. If the sail is too full in the middle, 'bags out' and produces a mighty, uncompromising pull like trying to hold on to an open umbrella in a gale there is too little

To pull on the downhaul tension, put one foot on the mastfoot and then straighten the leg rather than trying to pull with the arms. Tension it so the front of the sail is taught and solid, the head of the sail is flat and the leech a little loose.

Tuning

Having a basic knowledge of how a sail works helps you understand how altering its tensions and shape will affect its handling.

You can roughly divide the sail into two halves. The bottom half is the engine and the top half is the exhaust pipe. From the batten above the boom downward, the sail is designed to produce the power. Its shape, foiled like a wing, shouldn't change under load.

The top half of the sail is designed to change shape. Under load, the mast bends, the 'leech' (the sail's trailing edge) twists open and allows the air to escape. To a certain extent the modern sail is self-trimming. Because the top half can flex, it is outhaul. A sail that is too full gives you dire control problems as it gets windy, it can heave you over the front, drive the board sideways and stops you going upwind.

Boom Height
If you follow the sensible route and sign on to a course, the only aspect of tuning you have to worry about on day one is the height of the boom. Open up the clamp and slide the boom up and down within the sail cut-out. The favoured height at this stage is just below shoulder level. Measure it by holding the rig upright and standing right by the mast.

Boom height is crucial in that in that determines how you stand in relation to the rig. You should be able to ease back into a comfortably upright position with the arms more or less parallel with the water. If it is too low you will have to squat to exert any pressure against the rig. Too high, and you will find the rig has too much leverage over you and can all too easily pull you off balance. And having to stand with your hands constantly above your head is very tiring.

Check the boom on the bank. Just below shoulder height is perfect. (John Carter)

CHAPTER 3

UNDERSTANDING THE WIND

WIND AWARENESS

Keen windsurfers are obsessed with wind. They spend an almost unhealthy amount of time poring over weather forecasts, logging on to the Internet, checking webcams or just staring out of windows at bending branches.

Although you only need a very light breeze to get you started, thereafter you are forever craving more to allow you to tackle the next level. But like a capricious loved one, the wind comes and goes as it pleases, often letting you down, sometimes turning up unexpectedly. I write this from the Hawaiian island of Maui – the supposed wind capital of the world, where not even a leaf has moved for the past two weeks. You must accept that wind will bring joy and frustration in equal measure. There will be occasions when, having watched the boughs bending all day from your office window, you dash to the beach in the early evening, rig up with the speed of a whirling dervish, only for it to drop before your very eyes the moment you stick a toe in the water. On the other hand, there will be days when you are blessed with sun and winds of 17–27kt (force 5–6) and, after five hours of blissful blasting, you crawl from the water feeling more alive and invigorated than you ever thought possible.

Apart from controlling your life, the wind also influences your every move on the water. Its speed determines your speed and its direction decides and limits the directions you can sail in.

WIND STRENGTH

The language of wind strength to most seafarers, windsurfers and fishermen alike, is the Beaufort scale. It measures the wind on a scale of 1–11, with each number relating to a wind range – force 4, for example, represents a wind speed of 11–16kt.

You will quickly become familiar with the Beaufort scale if you hang about watery types, and you will find it very useful in helping you talk about and assess the suitability of the conditions. Should someone come off the water and say, 'it's blowing a good 6 out there', depending on your experience, you would know that either the wind was much too strong, or just perfect for practising jumps on your 80ltr board with a 5sq m sail.

Although the Beaufort scale is used throughout Europe, other countries, such as the USA, are more familiar with knots, so it is useful to understand both. A knot is one nautical mile per hour, which equals 1.1mph. Note that the wind speed figures

A wind of 1–6kt (force 1–2) is perfect for learning. (John Carter)

The Beaufort Scale

Wind force	Speed in knots	Conditions for windsurfing	Sea state
1–2	1–6	Perfect conditions for learning.	Wavelets with glass-like crests that do not break.
3	7–10	Still good for first-timers. There is enough pull in a bigger sail to get the board semi-planing – ideal for experimenting with the harness and the training footstraps.	Larger wavelets with crests that begin to break; glassy foam and occasional white horses.
4	11–16	It is still possible for ambitious first-timers to make good progress, as long as a very small sail is used. At this point, most large recreational boards fully release on to the plane.	Small waves with regular white horses.
5	17–21	Too windy for the beginner but perfect for practising waterstarts, carve gybes, freestyle and generally blasting around. All boards, bar the smallest wave boards, are now planing.	Moderate waves, which are longer with many white horses; some spray.
6	22–27	Waterstarting mandatory. Boards much over 120ltr will start to bounce out of control. Heavenly wind strength for the expert.	Large waves with extensive white foam crests; some spray.
7	28–33	Very windy. The expert dances a jig of delight and will be using a rig below 4.5sq m.	Choppy sea with white foam crests blown in streaks.
8	34–40	Gale force. As all other pleasure craft, seek shelter, the expert windsurfer, given the right size and design of board and sail, will be sailing along and turning in full control. The raw power of the wind means that things happen very quickly. There are, of course, serious safety concerns.	Relatively high waves with crest edges beginning to break into spindrift; foam forms noticeable streaks.
9	41–47	Severe gale. Experts still cutting it on sails as small as 3sq m and boards as small as 60ltr. Very hard to carry and launch the kit. In the likely event of a fall, the wind is strong enough to send board and rig tumbling away.	High waves with clear foam streaks, crests begin to tumble; visibility affected by sea spray.
10	48–55	Storm force. When forecasters warn of structural damage to trees and buildings, windsurfers can still be found out on the water but generally only in controlled situations. Professional racing, wave sailing and speed competitions have been staged in these conditions. Such winds are, however, very rare and the general advice is to stay firmly rooted to the land.	Very high waves with long, curved tumbling crests; large areas of streaked foam. Visibility severely affected by spray.

quoted on general, non-maritime, weather forecasts are usually in miles per hour.

My own version of the Beaufort scale, specially modified for windsurfers, is shown above.

WIND DIRECTION

If you come from a non-nautical background, you may regard wind just as something that dries the washing, blows people's hats off and ruins family picnics. You may not have thought of it as blowing from anywhere in particular. However, as a windsurfer, you always have to be aware of the direction.

Everything you do on the water, your manoeuvres and the courses you sail, is

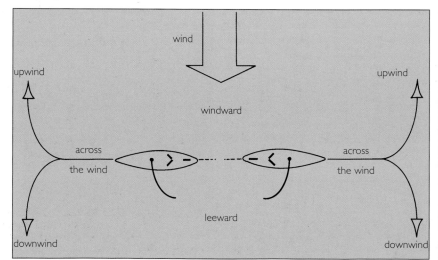

done in relation to the wind direction. So how do you know where the wind is coming from?

- Feel it just by the way it strikes your face or blows your hair.
- Look for the most obvious physical indicators such as smoke or flags. Your rig is a flag. Just hold it by the uphaul rope and it will flap downwind.
- Look at the water surface. The waves are generated by the wind and roll in the same direction. The water surface reveals the strength as well as the direction of the wind. You can see gusts moving across the water as dark patches. The darker the water, the stronger the wind. A glossy surface indicates a lull or 'hole' in the wind.

WIND TERMINOLOGY

In the first instance you should concentrate on just sailing across the wind. If you imagine the wind in the form of a big arrow, the course you begin by following is at 90 degrees to that arrow. From that point, any changes of direction you make are either upwind or downwind. Think of the wind as being generated by a big fan, upwind is moving towards the fan (the source of the wind), downwind is moving away from it.

You can sail in any direction apart from directly into the wind. The furthest upwind you can sail is about 45 degrees to the wind direction. Beyond that the sail stops producing any forward force. Unfortunately, the sight of bemused novices drifting gently backwards having just pointed the board towards home, oblivious to the fact that they are pointing into the wind, is all too familiar. Once you develop an instinctive feel for the wind direction, you will recognize the situation immediately and steer on to a new course.

Specific nautical terms for the various courses you can sail are described in Chapter 4.

A LEARNING WIND

The strength and direction of the wind has a massive influence on how easy you will find it to learn or improve. We cannot

With a big enough sail, the board will begin to plane in winds of 7–16kt (force 3–4). (John Carter)

At wind speeds of 17–27kt (force 5–6), sizeable waves begin to build on open water. This is the strength that most competent windsurfers dream about. They can use a small board and are perfectly powered up for all the planing manoeuvres. (John Carter)

At wind speeds of 34–47kt (gale force 8–9) windsurfers are the only sailing craft capable of handling both the force of the wind and the mountainous seas with any control. However, this is very much the domain of the extremely fit and highly skilled windsurfer. (John Carter)

At first, physical indicators such as flags help you determine the wind direction but ultimately you will know just by looking at the water. (John Carter)

control the weather but we can choose where to practise. Although subject to the same basic weather pattern, neighbouring venues can offer totally different conditions.

Gusts

The wind is constantly varying in speed and direction. However, the fewer obstacles, such as trees, buildings, mountains or headlands, there are in the way of it, the more constant it is. Gusty winds are frustrating for the beginner and expert alike. With the power in the sail always changing, it is very hard to settle into a comfortable, stable stance. Training at a venue that is open to the prevailing wind direction is invariably more fruitful – providing the wind isn't producing rough water.

Waves

Waves are one variable you can absolutely do without when coming to terms with the basics. Hence the majority of beginner schools are based on inland waters or in sheltered bays where the waves have had no distance to build.

Flat, sheltered water, a light, constant wind of 3–6kt (force 2), a wide board, and a small light rig – it is almost impossible not to learn to windsurf! (John Carter)

CHAPTER 4

THE BASICS

Windsurfing is the simplest form of sailing – in theory. There are no halyards, stays, or miles of rope, not even a rudder – just a board, a rig and you. You are the link, the transmission. You literally handle the power of the sail and direct it through your feet into the board.

The universal joint (UJ) at the bottom of the mast allows you not only to move the rig forward and back and from side to side but also to change the angle of the sail to the wind. Any moves you make with the rig alter how the power goes into the board and determine whether it goes straight or turns, accelerates or slows down.

WHAT MAKES A GOOD WINDSURFER?

Windsurfing is a dance. It is all about fluidity. The best dancers move as if they are treading on the finest china. They float across the floor and somehow conceal the fact that they are transferring weight from foot to foot. In some cases they are immensely strong, but that strength should never become visible or the dance is ruined.

Good windsurfers display similar characteristics. It is true that some, such as twelve-times world champion Bjorn Dunkerbeck, could easily be Arnold Schwarzenegger's body double, but most are relatively scrawny. What people like Cisco Goya and Josh Stone have in common, however, is the ability to turn themselves inside out. Agility, mobility and suppleness are far more important than strength, which is why, generally speaking, women make better windsurfers than men or at least learn more quickly. Women are naturally more supple, especially around the hips and waist – the area primarily

responsible for maintaining balance. Aware of their lack of raw power, they naturally seek out the most effective way of doing things (and they tend to listen to instructions – but that's another story!).

Men, meanwhile, regard strength as their greatest asset and use it. In light winds, it is possible to 'muscle' the rig into some sort of position where it makes the board go, so they develop problems with posture and other career-crippling habits from the outset.

Bjorn Dunkerbeck is massively powerful but it is his skill and general mobility rather than his muscles that took him to twelve consecutive world titles. (John Carter)

BALANCE

When windsurfing, the two fundamental goals are to control the power in the rig and to trim the board with the rig and your feet so it remains level on the water.

In the following pages, I will be offering specific guidelines about where best to place the hands and feet for each manoeuvre, which you may find useful when things aren't going entirely to plan. Windsurfing, however, should be less about rehearsing a series of mechanical steps and more about developing a few core skills that will serve you all the way to the top.

These essential skills come under the umbrella heading of 'balance', which in the context of windsurfing takes several forms – static balance, economy of movement, dynamic balance and rig balance.

Static Balance

Some people are naturally light-footed and supple around the hips, which allows them to shift their weight instinctively to remain upright on wobbly objects. However, anybody can improve their balance just by allowing the body to operate naturally as it does on dry land and observing the following advice.

- Keep your centre of gravity over your feet and stand naturally. Avoid the urge to stiffen, stick the bottom out, bend at the waist or look at the feet.
- Look up and keep your head still.
- Control of the 'core' of the body – the stomach and lower back – will help you to maintain your balance in difficult situations.
- Balance is not made easier by tensing every muscle – some people even try to grip the board with their feet. After five minutes they've got cramp in their calves and insteps. So just relax!
- Sudden and heavy foot movements set the board tipping; so hold your balance by moving something other than your feet. You can compensate by flexing the ankles, knees and hips.
- Avoid over-reaction. Try to keep all movements subtle and fluid.

Economy of Movement

The art of slick windsurfing lies in economy of movement. Sailing along in a constant wind, proficient windsurfers give the impression of being almost motionless. And when they do have to move – stepping to the other side of the board during a turn, for example – it all happens so

quickly and deftly that the board shows no reaction. By comparison, the whole board will react to every thrust and gyration of the less experienced sailor.

Moving your feet on a windsurfer is a special art. Unlike walking on dry land, on a windsurfer you need to develop the ability to move your foot without necessarily transferring your weight to it.

Imagine a line running from nose to tail along the 'centreline' (middle of the board). Concentrate on keeping the feet on or very near to that centreline. Tread on the edges and over you go. Think how you would walk over red-hot coals – probably by making yourself as light as possible, skipping on your toes and floating over the surface in the knowledge that to put any sudden pressure on the feet would result in severe pain and permanent scarring.

Dynamic Balance

Dynamic balance describes the skill of putting your body into a position where it can counterbalance the forces that build up as

Dynamic balance is the ability to move your body to anticipate and resist the forces thrown up by a change of direction – essential when windsurfing in high winds. (John Carter)

The art to develop is that of moving the feet without making sudden shifts of weight. (John Carter)

Yes, you are supposed to look where you are going but that doesn't stop you expressing yourself.
(John Carter)

the result of a sudden change of direction. Think of the move you make when cornering on a bicycle. A very basic instinct tells you that unless you bank over and lean to the inside, you will be catapulted to the outside of the bend. In windsurfing, dynamic balance really comes into play when you start going for turns on the plane. However, a key ingredient of dynamic balance is anticipation, and that applies from day one.

Anticipation
Anticipation is the skill of predicting a change in speed or direction before it happens. Novices in all motion sports tend to be reactive – they wait for something to happen and then react to it, by which time it is too late, they are already off-balance and playing a game of catch-up. Anticipation is an essential skill in windsurfing as the environment is constantly changing. In rough water and fickle winds you

must read the conditions ahead and move your body before the wave or gust arrives.

The Head
In all balance sports the head plays a key role. If the head stays still, so will the rest of the body. When it comes to motion, the body tends to follow the head. Where you look is where you end up. If you turn your head to the direction you want to move towards, you stay in balance. Close your eyes or look at your feet and you grind to a halt.

Vision
Vision is vital to all aspects of windsurfing. As well as being crucial to balance and general orientation, there is also a wider issue. Windsurfing takes place in a highly unpredictable environment. In all balance sports beginners will inevitably stare fixedly at their feet. Nonetheless, you must try from the outset to extend your vision to

spot the gusts and lulls on the water ahead. Later on you will need to look even further. You may have noticed how proficient wave sailors appear to turn and head off for no apparent reason. Then suddenly you will see them in exactly the right position to catch the biggest wave of the day. With their eyes scanning the whole ocean, they spotted the swell way off on the horizon.

Rig Balance and Control
Whether you are a first-timer or a freestyling wizard, how you handle the rig and control its power will determine, above all else, your levels of success. The reason you don't actually need exquisite natural balance to reach a high standard is that you have the boom to hang on to. You are leaning against the power of the sail and using your body as a counterweight.

To stay in balance, be sure to regulate

It is the instinctive push-pull of the arms to adjust the sail and the power that holds you upright.
(John Carter)

the power the sail produces by changing its angle to the wind, and move your body towards and away from the sail to adjust how much weight you are leaning against it.

You will feel the power in your hands, and through a simple push-pull motion with the shoulders you can catch more wind to increase power or spill wind to slow down.

So, as your initiation draws near, try to free your mind of all preconceptions. It's not difficult. You won't spend most of the time falling off. Attack it with energy and controlled aggression and you will triumph.

THE CARRY AND LAUNCH

'Let the wind do the work', is a maxim that you can apply to just about every aspect of

windsurfing. If you go with the force and let the wind pull you into position, life is easy. The moment you start to fight the wind, it becomes a great deal more difficult – and never is that more true than for the simple act of carrying board and rig.

Carrying the Board
The following will aid your well-being.

• If you hold the board on your upwind side, a gust can catch it and blow it on top of you, so carry it on your downwind side.
• Hold the board so either nose or tail is facing into wind. This presents less of the board to the wind and prevents it from being blown around.
• Watch out for the fin(s)! It sticks out quite a way and is not only fragile but

can be an offensive weapon to passers-by.
• The board will feel light and manageable if you carry it from the middle but totally unwieldy and heavy if you do not.

Launching
How you actually launch depends on the venue and conditions. If it is a shallow shelving beach with no rocks, you can connect board and rig at the water's edge and push them in together. If it is more steeply shelving or littered with stones that could damage the board and sail, carry them in separately. Left to its own devices, the board will swiftly drift away on the wind, so carry the rig into the water first, then fetch the board and connect them together.

The rig will support itself if you hold the mast and/or the boom from the middle and let the wind blow under it. This method is ideal for carrying the rig downwind. (John Carter)

To carry the rig across or into wind, place one hand on the mast, the other on the underside of the boom and lift the whole rig over your head, keeping the mastfoot pointing into the wind. Shift it around on your head until it feels balanced. With the wind blowing under it, the rig is virtually weightless. (John Carter)

The board is too wide for you to tuck under your arm like a surfboard. A popular method is to roll it on to its edge and, standing by the underside of the board, reach over with the back hand, grab the top of the daggerboard and lift it, using the spare hand to balance the board. If there is a central fin instead of a daggerboard, stand by the deck, reach over, grab the fin with your backhand, and lift it, using the spare hand to balance the board. Some entry-level boards have a special carrying handle moulded into the deck. (John Carter)

To launch the board and rig together, stand between them. Lift the tail of the board with one hand, hold the top of the boom with the other and shove them into the water. (John Carter)

To connect the board and rig, tip the board on its side to plug in the mastfoot. (John Carter)

Believe it or not, there is even a technique for this. Most UJs are made of stiff rubber, so rather than trying to bend them, it is easier to tip the board on its side. If out of your depth, you will have to sit on the board and just use a bit of strength to bend it into place.

There are various systems for connecting the mastfoot to the mast base, so familiarize yourself with them on dry land. It usually involves putting a pin into the mast base and depressing a locking button.

With the next stage in mind, ensure that the nose of the board is facing away from the beach and the rig is on the downwind side.

Although it is tempting at this point just to lunge for the sail and get going, try to keep a check on your enthusiasm. Remember that you have no idea of how to turn round or stop. You must learn to get on, raise the rig and turn around on the spot before powering up the sail and getting into a sailing position.

Getting On

You will be sick of hearing it but 'keep your weight over the centreline' will ring out like a mantra during these early stages. If you try to get on just by clambering up on the nearest bit of board, grabbing the edges for support, you will end up looking like a seal trying to slither its way on to a slimy rock. However, if you keep your hands and shoulders over the middle of the board, you'll pop up like a dolphin.

If your board has a retractable daggerboard, rotate it into the 'down' position before you get on. If using a wide board, you will be pleasantly surprised by how stable it feels. Even so, be sure to grab the uphaul rope before standing as you then have something to balance against.

Uphauling

Pulling the rig from the water is easy if done correctly. The legs contain the strongest muscles, so let them do the heavy work while keeping the back straight.

When the rig is partially raised, the end of the boom is still in the water. If the wind catches the sail, it will be trapped and try to blow the sail back down. Once the end of the boom is clear, the sail just flaps impotently. The remedy lies in subtle aggression – the quicker you pull the rig out, the less chance the wind has to catch it.

At the other extreme, if you just lean back and heave with all your might, the end of the boom can suddenly fly clear, whereupon all resistance disappears and over you go. As you pull it up the last few inches, anticipate that drop in force by moving your weight inboard.

Neutral

This key position has also been known at different times in windsurfing history as the 'secure' or 'start' position. In neutral, the sail generates little or no power, giving you a base from which to practise your balance without going anywhere. It is the position from which you turn the board round and the one you return to whenever you want a breather or need to orientate yourself again. The goal is to end up standing upright with your back to the wind, as relaxed as you would be on solid ground; the board lying across the wind and rig flapping downwind.

Keep the head up, hold the mast with either one or both hands and extend the arms to keep it away from you. It is very important to stand as far away from the rig as possible. Whether sailing along, turning or just waiting in neutral, if you stand too close to the rig, you have no room to react and are especially vulnerable to sudden wobbles or changes in sail pressure.

Turning Round

From the neutral position with the hands on the mast, if you lean the rig against the wind, the board will turn under the sail. In order to complete a 180-degree turn to face the opposite direction, either the nose or the tail has to pass through the eye of the wind and you must also turn your body through 180 degrees.

You can turn either way. If you swing the rig over the tail, the nose turns upwind and you step around the front of the mast to take up position on the new side. If you swing the rig over the nose, the nose turns downwind and you step around behind the mast.

In windsurfing, this moment where the board passes through the wind and you step around the mast is known as 'transition'. All the previous balance tips apply: take small, light steps; keep the rig at arm's length; hold the head high; but perhaps the most significant in this case is speed. You

are very vulnerable when your feet are off the centreline in mid-transition; so the quicker you can get around the mast and back in the neutral position, the greater your chances of instant success.

There is a basic and wholly understandable instinct that tells you to go very slowly and do nothing that might change things for the worse. Ignore that instinct and get on with it – with controlled haste. Hesitation and playing safe are desperately destructive habits that kill any chance of mastering high winds and smaller boards.

No matter which way the wind is blowing, approach from the opposite side to the rig and place your hands on the centreline just behind the mastfoot.

Climbing-on Sequence *(John Carter)*

Pull yourself up until your shoulders are over your hands and your weight is over the middle of the board.

Wind Direction

Leaving your hands where they are, pull yourself up on to your knees, and bring them also on to the centreline.

Still kneeling, grab the bottom of the uphaul rope …

Wind
Direction

… and place your feet on the centreline, about shoulder-width apart, on either side of the mastfoot. Stay fully crouched for stability.

Keeping the back and arms straight, straighten the legs. As the rig comes up, the water will drain off and make it even lighter.

Wind Direction

←

With the legs now extended, pull the rig out the rest of the way by working your hands up to the top of the rope.

Grab the mast just below the boom with both hands to take up the neutral position. Swing the rig forward and back until it is at right angles to the board. Make a body check – head up, back straight, the rig held at arm's length, all joints slightly flexed and your weight spread over the whole foot, not just the toes. This is the all important 'neutral' or 'secure' position.

Wind Direction

⟵

Turning round on the spot in both directions, upwind and downwind, is the very best form of practice. You will learn how the board moves on the water and where you can and cannot put your feet. You will also get a feeling for the weight and balance of the rig and begin to understand that the less you struggle, the easier it is. But best of all is the fact that all this is taking place within a spit of the shore, so you can practise in total confidence before powering off into the deep blue yonder.

Catching the Wind in the Sail

If you hold the rig by the mast in the secure position, the wind effectively misses the sail. It just passes over both sides and makes it flap like a flag.

When you grab the boom from the middle and pull it towards you, one side of the sail is presented to the wind. It then fills with wind and produces power. The trick to getting into the sailing position relies on making sure that your body is in a position where it can counterbalance the

force as the sail powers up and that the rig is held at an angle where it drives the board forward in a straight line.

Everyone gets pulled over forwards when they first try to power up the sail. Most beginners are reluctant to lean back because until they have some experience, they don't trust the rig to hold them. There is also a huge temptation to grab the boom too soon because it looks like a railing you can steady yourself on. The boom, however, is a nervous accelerator

From the neutral position, tilt the rig towards the back of the board and lean it against the wind.

Wind
Direction

←

The tail and rig come together and the nose turns towards the wind. Note how the windsurfer holds the rig at arm's length throughout the turn.

Turning Round Sequence *(John Carter)*

With the rig over the back of the board and the nose facing directly into the wind, start stepping around the mast, keeping the feet close to the mastfoot and away from the edges.

Wind
Direction

Move the feet back on to the centreline and keep leaning the rig against the wind until the board is once again across the wind. You are back in neutral and the 180-degree turn is complete.

pedal. Grab it and you change the angle of
the sail, catch the wind and power up. If
you are already leaning forward, it doesn't
take much to tip you over.

The advantage of starting in a light wind
with a smaller sail is that the pull is gentle
so you can very gradually get used to easing your weight back to resist it.

Making Room

I have mentioned this already, but now it
is especially relevant. If you stand too close
to the rig, you are blind to your surroundings and powerless to use your levers. It is
very important to step back from the rig
before you pull on the power and then
hold it away from you on extended arms.

The Balance Point

The key to a smooth getaway is to bring
the rig to the point where it balances itself
before powering it up. Tilt the mast into
wind, find the point where you can let go
and the rig will hang there for a second
(this will be the key to slick sail transitions
later on). The greater the force of the
wind, the further you have to tilt it. The
aim to begin with is to hold it vertical. If
you let it drop even a few degrees downwind, the weight of the rig alone is enough
to pull you off balance on to your toes.

STANCE

From my privileged position overlooking
Camp One beach on the Hawaiian island
of Maui, I am watching two of the very
best sailors in the world.

Ricardo Campello, the teenage
freestyle sensation from Venezuela, sets
his boom unusually high and hangs off it
with the arms and body totally straight. He
is sparring with twelve-times overall world
champion Bjorn Dunkerbeck. From many
years of flying around race courses holding
down hugely powerful race sails, Bjorn has
developed a more compact and solid
stance – slightly crouched with arms and

*Despite the difference in weight, the lighter woman manages to topple the
heavier man because she keeps her back straight, drops her weight on to her
heels and so can use her whole body to resist him. Because he has bent
forward at the waist, the only muscles he can use are those in his toes. This is
not efficient yet this is how many try to oppose the force in the sail.
(John Carter)*

*From neutral, release the front hand from the mast. Look ahead and identify
a point across the wind to head for.*

Getting Going Sequence *(John Carter)*

Now grab the front of the boom with the front hand …

Wind
Direction

… and release the other hand. Give yourself a little more room by placing the front foot alongside the mast and the back foot about 45cm (18in) behind it.

Pull the rig across your body towards the wind until the rig balances itself and you can see the nose of the board through the sail. As you do so, turn the shoulders and hips to favour the direction that you are about to take off in.

Take hold of the middle of the boom with the back hand and pull it towards you. As the sail catches the wind and starts pulling, bend the knees slightly and ease your weight against it. The board will glide away – you're windsurfing. Relax and enjoy!

Stance (John Carter)

- *The head looks forward and upwind to pick the route and read the water for gusts and lulls.*
- *The arms are extended or just slightly bent.*
- *The hands are shoulder-width apart and find a position on the boom where there is equal pressure on both arms (if the back arm is over-working, move both hands back and vice versa). The fingers are draped over the boom. There is no advantage to be gained from squeezing it. The shoulders and upper body are parallel to the boom.*
- *The bottom is tucked in so the hips are inboard of the shoulders. The hips are also parallel to the boom so you get a feeling of pulling directly against the power of the sail.*
- *The feet stand shoulder-width apart behind the mastfoot. The back foot is across the centreline whilst the front foot is angled slightly forward in the direction of travel.*
- *The rig is upright, in perfect balance with the sailor's weight and pulled in just enough to stop the sail flapping.*

legs a little bent to absorb the bumps and gusts.

Neither is wrong. Each has simply developed the most appropriate posture for his weight, dimensions and the type of windsurfing he is doing. You will eventually do the same.

The strength of the wind naturally influences your stance but the basic elements stay the same, which is why it is so important to get into good habits from the start.

The picture above illustrates a model stance for light winds and explains the role of the body parts. Keep that model in mind but at the same time focus on what you wish to achieve, such as keeping the rig still and riding the board flat on the water, rather than slotting, military-style, into a fixed position.

Many pick up on certain instructions such as 'keep your arms straight' and lock them out like a couple of iron rods, forgetting why they are doing it. The general aim is to keep the rig at arm's length so you have better leverage over it and room to react. But the arms should also be free to bend and stretch in order to balance and change the angle of the sail.

Remember, the ultimate goal is to develop good posture and become:

- Balanced, stable and relaxed.
- Free-moving with all joints slightly flexed.
- Able to transfer weight from one foot to another

Power Control

Think of the rig as a door opening and closing. Your front hand (the one nearest the front of the board) is the hinge and the back hand holds the handle. If you open the door by pushing the back hand away from you, the wind will escape and so reduce the power. If you close the door by pulling the back hand towards you, the wind is trapped and the power increases.

That is a simplistic view of a complex situation but in the very beginning it helps you to see the rig as two-dimensional. As you feel the power build in the sail, a common error is to let the whole rig fall downwind, at which point you get pulled on to your toes and are forced to take up the classic 'backside to the heavens' beginner's posture. But if you concentrate on keeping the front hand, the hinge, still and allow the rig to pivot around it, the mast stays upright and you can maintain your stance.

The reality, as your responses to the

sail's changing pressure become more instinctive, is that you will find yourself using both arms to alter the rig angle with a push-pull action. If you need to lose power suddenly, push the back arm away at the same time as pulling the front hand in.

Sheeting Angle

There are moments in every novice's life when, despite a healthy breeze and what you consider to be a model sailing stance, you remain motionless. There are two possible reasons. You are either lying head to wind, in which case the sail produces no forward force, or you are holding the sail at the wrong angle to the wind.

The optimum sail ('sheeting') angle depends on your sailing course. Think about exposing the maximum sail area to the wind. Sailing upwind, therefore, hold the rig close to the board so the foot of the sail is more or less over the centreline. As you head away from the wind, open the sail so the end of the boom is further and further away from the board. But how do you know whether you have got the right angle? By feel.

As you 'sheet in' (pull in the sail) with the back hand, the power gradually increases until you reach a maximum. If you keep pulling in after that, the power gradually lessens. Effectively, you are 'over sheeting', that is, stopping the wind flowing evenly over the sail and causing it to stall. This is a perfectly legitimate way of reducing power at high speeds and during extreme manoeuvres. But in the early stages, because there is relatively little pressure in the sail, it is all too easy to pull it in too far. If you do become that static object in a sea of activity, this is often the reason. The remedy is to 'sheet out' (open the sail) until you feel the power increase.

If you stop and you have no idea why, the fail-safe measure is always to return to the neutral position and start again.

The Still Rig

If you can move the sail to cope with the gusts and lulls and so avoid the energy-sapping penalties of dropping the rig or falling in, your sailing time and general enjoyment immediately double. But before complacency sets in, let me

When the wind drops suddenly, the automatic reaction as you fall back is to try to pull yourself up on the boom. However, if you keep pulling, you will stall the sail, kill all the power and heave it down over your head.

Instead, give a quick tug with the back hand to create a burst of power then immediately push it away again. At the same time, leave the mast upright and throw the hips forward inboard under the boom. (John Carter)

immediately move the goal posts. Moving the rig, although still necessary in a crisis, is essentially a bad habit. The aim now is to keep the rig upright and still so it produces a constant flow of power into the board. To do that you must:

• Look upwind to spot the wind on the water and anticipate the rise or drop in pressure.
• Turn your body into a mobile counterbalance.

This is all about your hips and bottom. They represent your centre of gravity and therefore your ballast. Like a pendulum, they swing towards and away from the board. Sailing along, you see a glassy patch of water ahead revealing a lull in the wind. The second you feel the pressure in the sail decrease, push the hips forward to bring your weight more over the centreline of the board. As the wind picks up again, swing the hips out, away from the

If you get pulled forward on to your toes, ease the power by opening the sail with the back hand …

Wind
Direction

… before standing up straight, pulling the rig upright and setting off again. (John Carter)

Wind
Direction

The Beachstart; when the mast is upright you can pull yourself up under the boom. (John Carter)

grasp – mastfoot steering and power control through mast angle.

Mastfoot Steering

Standing in the water upwind of the board, you can push and pull the nose into position using the rig. As long as the daggerboard or central fin is removed, the board pivots around the fin. So, by pushing down on the boom or the mast and applying pressure into the mastfoot, you push the nose downwind; by lifting up on the boom or mast, you bring the nose upwind.

New Power Control

When the rig is tilted over at an angle, less area is exposed to the wind so it produces less power than when upright. Using this principle will enable you to get the rig to lift you on to the board both for the beachstart and, later, the waterstart (see Chapter 6). You will master the beachstart in a matter of hours if you:

- Step forward on the board, not on to the tail.
- Never use the boom as a bar to heave yourself up on. Do just the opposite. Extend the front hand towards the mastfoot to produce the power to lift you on.

Stepping on to the board is just like climbing a step – you have to get your weight over your bent knee, then extend the leg and step up.

STOPPING

In fast, sliding, balance sports such as skiing, ice-skating or windsurfing, the beginner is not so much inhibited by the prospect of going fast as the fear of not being able to stop. When windsurfing in light winds, you are unlikely to break any speed records but all it takes is a sudden gust and the bank or nearest solid object approaches very much faster than expected.

Initially, there are three ways to slow down and stop on a windsurfer. The one you choose depends on the severity of the situation.

- Gently. Let go of the back hand, the sail will de-power and the board will slide

board. All the time the shoulders and the rig stay still.

THE BEACHSTART

This is a far more stylish, quicker and ultimately easier way of leaving the shore than wading out, scrambling aboard and pulling up the rig. In the beachstart, you stand next to the board holding the rig and step up straight into your sailing position.

You can learn to beachstart as soon as you have the most basic power control. In fact, this is a good move to practise early

on because it forces you to work on your power control. The only limiting factors are the venue and the wind.

As the name suggests, you need a beach or at least a non-rocky shoreline where you can stand comfortably in thigh- to waist-deep water. A wind of 7–10kn (force 3) is ideal but it needs to be solid right into the beach so you have enough power in the sail to lift you on. The ideal direction is parallel with the shore although it is possible to launch in any wind direction.

The beachstart is straightforward although there are two new concepts to

With the board lying across the wind in thigh-deep water, position yourself about 1m (3ft) upwind of the tail. Angle the rig down over your head to control the power.

Wind Direction

Lift the back foot in the middle of the board.

Roll the shoulders forward, extend the arms to get the rig as high as possible and when your knee is over your foot ...

... extend the back leg, and step the front leg forward so you end up in your sailing position.

Beachstart Sequence *(John Carter)*

gently to a stop.
- More urgently. Check the water is clear downwind before grabbing the uphaul rope and lowering the rig into the water. The rig then acts like a drag chute and the board will stop almost immediately.
- Critical. Again, make sure no one is downwind of you but this time just let the rig go, fall on to it and use your weight to sink it.

The fourth method, and the one employed by most windsurfers travelling at speed, is to steer sharply into wind. By turning, you usually avoid the trouble and by coming into wind, the sail de-powers and the force of the wind stops you dead in your tracks. However, there are two good reasons why you cannot use that method at present. First, because in a light wind, a big board turns into wind quite

slowly; second, because I haven't told you how to steer yet!

Coming Ashore
You can lower the rig into the water as you approach the beach, drop on to your knees and step off in the shallows. However, given a shallow shelving bank or beach, it is far slicker and more efficient to do a beachstart in reverse. Sheet out to slow down and as you drift into thigh-

If you drop the rig into the water, the board will stop almost immediately, just make sure that there is no one directly downwind of you. (John Carter)

As with normal sailing, the key to steering and manoeuvring comes from rig control and keeping your distance from the rig. Whatever move you make with the rig, make the opposite move with your body. (John Carter)

deep water, step off to windward (the upwind side) holding the rig and then push it out holding the tail with one hand and the boom with the other (the same technique you used for pushing it in).

To avoid damaging yourself or the board, retract the daggerboard and then get off before the fin smacks the bottom because you never know what lies on the seabed in the form of rocks, supermarket trolleys or other spiky debris. Step off gently, on no account be tempted to jump.

STEERING AND TURNING

In principle, sailing and steering in light winds is wonderfully simple. The sail has an imaginary spot where all the forces are concentrated. It is the point where the sail pulls from and when you are sailing, it should lie between your hands — that way the pressure is equally distributed between both arms.

To steer towards the wind, tilt the rig back by stretching the back arm towards the tail and pulling the front arm into the chest. (John Carter)

Wind Direction

To steer away from the wind, tilt the rig forward by stretching the front arm towards the nose and bending the back arm into the chest. (John Carter)

The board has a central pivot point, which in light winds is represented by the daggerboard or central fin. As if a nail had been driven through the deck, it is the point about which the board turns. If you hold the rig upright so the power lies directly over the board's pivot point, you will track in a straight line. Tilt it forward or back and you will turn and keep turning until either you bring the rig upright again or the board reaches the extremes of upwind or downwind.

Sailing across the wind, if you tilt the rig towards the nose, it will push the nose downwind so you 'bear away' (steer downwind). If you tilt the rig towards the tail, it will push the tail downwind so you 'head up' (steer upwind).

Short, fat boards have less resistance to turning than the traditional long boards but how speedily you get them to steer depends on the size of sail, the strength of the wind and on how aggressively you move the rig. The more power you have in your hands, the faster you can turn. As you get more confident, you can slide the hands up or down the boom in order to throw the rig further forward or back.

This is very nearly as simple as it sounds; however every time you move the rig, it pulls from a different angle. To stay in balance, whatever movement you make with the rig, you have to make an opposite movement with the body.

When you tilt the rig back to head up, the pressure tries to pull you over the tail, so lean your weight towards the nose to compensate. When you lean the rig forward to bear away, the sail threatens to pull you over the nose, so lower the body, ease the weight on to your back foot and brace against the front leg.

SAILING COURSES

Windsurfers have done their best over the years to substitute 'nautical-speak' with the language of the common man. However, those crusty old sea captains knew a thing or two and when it comes to describing the different directions you sail in, or 'points of sailing' as they are better known, things have changed little since the days of Horatio Nelson. As you get into the sport, you will find that instructions about what to do and when are all described in relation to these points of sailing. From Honolulu to Birmingham, descriptions relative to the wind are constant.

Every point of sailing poses a slightly different challenge but on a big board in light, non-planing conditions, most people manage to steer a course that takes them all in on their first or second day.

As you steer both upwind and downwind, the vital skill is to become ever more aware of the wind direction and therefore the course you are on. So many people complain that on their one and only windsurfing experience (usually on holiday and without a tutor), they could go out but were unable to get back. When I hear such stories, I suspect immediately that they set off oblivious to the fact they were sailing almost dead downwind; so when they turned round and headed for home, they were pointing directly into wind and so just drifted backwards.

There are many ways to spot the wind direction from your sailing position apart from looking at flags and the angle of the waves.

- If sailing upwind on a close reach, you will feel the wind on your face. If sailing downwind on a broad reach or a run you will feel it on your back.
- The most reliable way is to feel which way the rig is pulling you. If the pull is forward towards the nose, you are sailing downwind. If the pull is sideways, you are sailing across or upwind.

The Changing Stance
The principles of your stance are the same for all the points of sailing except a run.

Your aim is to face the pull of the sail so your hips and shoulders are always parallel to the boom. But because the sheeting angle is different for each course, your body angle to the board will be different.

The Tack

'Tacking' describes the act of turning upwind through the eye of the wind. As the nose passes through the wind, you walk around the mast to take up your stance on the new side. As you set off again from a new neutral position, you will be facing the opposite direction, the wind will hit the other side of the sail and your hands will be on the other side of the boom.

The simplest form of the tack is to sail across the wind, return to the neutral position with one or both hands on the mast and then turn the board round by leaning the rig against the wind and swinging it over the tail until you end up in a neutral position on the new side (see page 55).

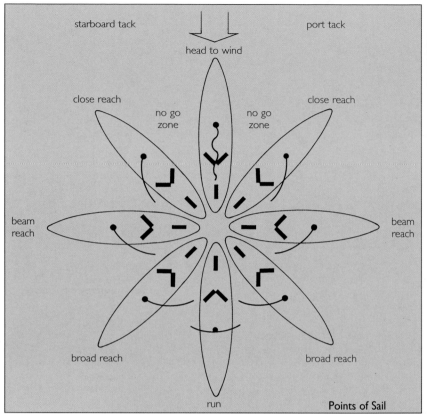

Points of Sail

On a close reach, the sail is sheeted in close to the centreline, so your hips and shoulders also face more parallel to the board. Concentrate on directing that force through the feet and against the daggerboard or central fin, which resists it and turns it into forward motion.

Wind Direction

On a broad reach, the sheeting angle is more open with the end of the boom further away from the board. The rig pulls you forwards so your hips and shoulders turn more towards the nose to face that pull. With the wind from behind and the whole sail area exposed to it, this is your fastest point of sailing. Even in a light breeze, resist the extra forward pull by bracing against the front leg and bending the back leg. (John Carter)

Once you get into the swing of things, you will notice that if you are using a small sail, the board reacts slowly and the whole process takes some time. You can speed things up by steering into wind from the sailing position before stepping around the mast, as illustrated below and overleaf.

Tacking Upwind

The nautical jargon can get just a tad confusing at this point. The 'tack' or 'tacking', as just described, is the act of turning upwind through the wind. However, 'tacking', otherwise known as 'beating', also describes the act of making multiple turns and sailing a zigzag course to reach a point directly upwind.

Getting to a point upwind of where you started is like being awarded with a certificate to say that you have made that essential transition from passenger to pilot. When you are not sailing along, then you and the board are just like all the other flotsam and jetsam. Do nothing and you will drift downwind until you are washed up on the lee shore, from where you have to endure the walk of shame back to your start point. However, once you begin to maintain and even make ground against the wind, it proves not only that you are doing more sailing than swimming but also that you are aware of the wind direction and deliberately sailing a close-reaching course.

Sadly, the upwind walk of shame is a recurring penalty. Every time you grope for the next level – more wind, a bigger sail, a smaller board – the sailing to floundering ratio drops again and you return to jetsam mode.

Tacking upwind is like trying to make ground up a steep hill. If you try the direct route, you slip back. Instead, you set off on a diagonal track, go so far, turn around and follow a diagonal track in the other direction. How many zigzags you make and the length of each zig and zag depends on the width of the slope and the distance to your destination. If you fall, you swiftly lose a lot of ground and all the hard work is undone.

Sailing is the same. Upwind, you go at half the speed and cover twice the distance. It is also a far greater test of skill – with less forward drive in the sail, the

sheeting angles have to be more precise. You also need to be much more aware of the course you are sailing, as the board will only travel within a certain angle of the wind direction. Sailing fast downwind demands a degree of skill but if you just hold the sail up, you will get blown along – until you fall, at which point you will still get blown along but just a little more slowly.

The trick to beating lies in finding that 'close-hauled' track – in other words the closest track possible to the wind or the limit of the 'no-go zone'. There is no set angle; it depends on the design of the board and the strength of the wind. The more sideways resistance a board can offer, the closer to the wind it sails. This is why boards with big daggerboards and Formula racing boards with their huge fins

point higher than recreational boards with small fins and perhaps no daggerboard. Given a skilled rider, the stronger the wind, the higher the board will point.

Tacking upwind is all done by feel. Start off as normal by sailing across the wind before steering up into wind and straightening out on to a close reach; then steer upwind again and try a closer reach. Eventually you arrive at a point where everything begins to stall. The sail suddenly feels heavy in the hands and yet produces no forward drive; and the board, rather than moving smoothly through the water, starts to 'crab' sideways. You have edged into the 'no-go' area. To resume normal service, tilt the rig forward and bear away a few degrees until the sail starts to drive the board forwards. Then head up again and try to find that fine line between sailing and stalling. Carry on for as long as the the mood takes you or the width of the sailing area allows before tacking and repeating the process.

Beating upwind in a confined space is the best training exercise at this level. Sailing close to the wind makes you

Beam reach. When sailing across the wind, angle the rig back to steer upwind. Keep pulling in with the back hand and you will turn all the way up into wind.

Tack Sequence (John Carter)

With the nose facing into the wind and pointing directly at the waves, the board will stop and the pressure in the sail will drop. Release the back hand and grab the mast. The front hand can either grab the mast or hang free.

Step gingerly around the mast while, at the same time, angling the rig back and swinging it over the tail.

Move the feet into their new start positions on either side of the mast and keep leaning the rig against the wind until the board is lying across the wind once more.

Step back into the sailing position, power up the rig and return from whence you came.

especially aware of sail trim and wind direction, whilst the tacks themselves improve your footwork and general mobility. Best of all, just the knowledge that you can sail upwind and stay out of trouble does wonders for your confidence.

Running with the Wind

As the name suggests, 'running' is the point of sailing that exactly follows the wind direction. Having steered right off the wind, turn to face the front of the board and place the feet either side of the centreline. Then hold the rig at right angles to the board with the hands in the middle of the boom.

This is a very unnatural course. First, it is slow and the sail works very inefficiently. The wind no longer passes over like a wing but is interrupted by it and so blows the board along like a paper boat. Moreover, it is unstable. With the feet either side of the centreline, even the wide boards are considerably more nervous. Throw a gusty wind and few waves into the mix and your balance will be tested to the limit.

So why do it? To be honest, some people have been windsurfing for ten years without being on a run and neither are they likely to. However, in a light wind on flat water, it is fairly straightforward and might be useful if you need to manoeuvre in a confined space.

During a basic gybe, you turn momentarily on to a run but apart from that, there is little to recommend it. On the downwind leg of a race, in winds strong enough to plane, most elect to zigzag to the buoy via a series of broad reaches rather than run directly to it. Although this involves travelling further, you will be planing (it is very difficult to make the board plane on a run) and therefore moving at more than twice the speed.

Gybing

The 'gybe' or 'jibe' is the opposite turn to the tack in that it takes you downwind through the wind. However, before you have a go, you should first get the hang of sailing upwind.

Why gybe when a tack will help you gain ground against the wind? Well, you might be sailing downwind deliberately and want to turn from a broad reach on

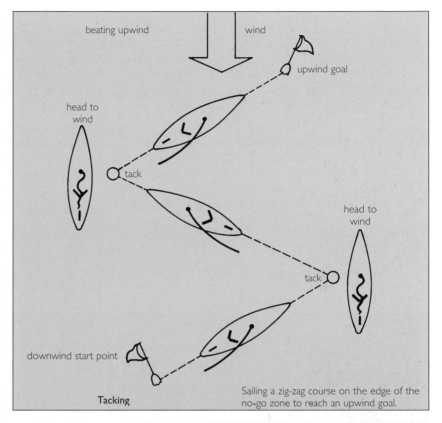

Tacking

Sailing a zig-zag course on the edge of the no-go zone to reach an upwind goal.

Running with the wind can be useful but it is the slowest and least exciting part of sailing. With the feet placed either side of the centreline, it is also the least stable. (John Carter)

Wind Direction

one side to a broad reach on the other. If you tack, you will have to turn the board through 270 degrees; if you gybe, you go through just 90 degrees.

However, the main reason to gybe is that it is a more thrilling and an altogether more natural move. The force is always with you. As you bear away downwind, the board accelerates and becomes more stable. During the transition, the feet stay behind the mast and just swap places, avoiding that tortuous walk around the nose. Through the whole transition the board is still being blown along. Even in light wind, there is a tremendous sensation of movement. In stronger winds, the planing carve gybe is so exciting (and frustrating) that it is now a global obsession, which is why I have devoted an entire chapter to it (see Chapter 8).

Like the basic tack, you can gybe by returning to the neutral position with one or both hands on the mast and then swing the rig over the nose to end up across the wind facing the other way. Again, like the basic tack, this is easy and effective but a bit sluggish.

If you feel confident about the whole thing, you can move straight on to a rather more advanced variation where you sail into the gybe and make better use of the rig to speed up the rotation.

BEACH AND WATERCRAFT

It had been a long, hard day. My charges had been through the whole beginner syllabus in seven hours and had done everything necessary to be granted what was then called the Level One certificate –

except one thing – they had not listened to the mandatory safety lecture. So I led them off into the debriefing chamber and spouted on for the best part of an hour about tides, fronts, depressions, the dangers of offshore winds, shipping lanes, rip currents, tsunamis, and so on.

Suddenly, I was struck by the absurdity of the whole situation. Here we were, miles away from the nearest coast, at a gravel pit where it was no more than perhaps 80m to the far bank. If they could not sail back to base, the worst-case scenario was that they would have to walk back along the grassy bank. It was a mild day with light winds, a rescue boat in constant attendance; yet there I was, striking the fear of God into them by graphically describing a list of impending natural disasters.

Across the wind, lean the rig forward and pull in the back hand to bear away downwind. Stay low, push off the front leg to help the nose turn downwind.

Gybe Sequence *(John Carter)*

Dead downwind, open out the back hand so the rig is at right angles to the board and place the feet either side of the centreline with the toes facing forward.

Wind Direction

Place the back hand on the mast, release the front hand, and swing the rig over the nose.

As the board turns through the wind, place the feet on the centreline once more.

Wind Direction

The board is still moving so there is no need to linger in the neutral position. Just wait until the board is across the wind, then pull the rig across the body, power up the sail, and accelerate away.

Windsurfing is an incredibly safe sport and why I urge everyone to start their career in an official school is because those potentially unsafe variables such as wind and sea conditions, and the safety issue in general, are taken care of, leaving you free to develop your skills.

There is nothing very exciting about the subject of safety and, for it to mean anything, it must be relevant. Throughout the book, I shall be feeding in cautionary tales as and where appropriate. Next, however, we shall look at situations that are outside the normal common-sense parameters.

Keep your hands above your head as you fall and as you surface again to protect yourself from the falling mast. (John Carter)

Falling In

The joyous result of experimentation. Everyone does it, from novice to freestyle wizard. Almost all of the time you just get wet and surface with a smile. There are, however, a few situations to be wary of.

- The parachute effect. If you let go of the rig as you fall backwards, it can momentarily turn itself into a parachute and float down more slowly than you. There is a slim chance that it could smack you on the head just as you surface after your dive. The remedy is to hold your hands over your head as you

fall and keep them there as you come back up again.

- Getting caught under the sail. If you fall in backwards holding the rig and surface to find yourself under the sail, do not try to burst your way through the sail like a leaping salmon, just swim calmly to the side. Clear air is at most 1.8m (6ft) away. On flat water, there is usually an air pocket under the sail.
- Shallow water. Be very wary of falling or deliberately jumping off head or feet first, as the water may be shallower than you thought. Instead, try and land flat so no part of you makes sudden contact with the bottom.

The safest way to leave your equipment on the shore is with the mast tip pointing down and the board, still connected, lying upside-down on top. (John Carter)

On the Beach

Boards that have been casually abandoned on the shore are a potential menace, usually to innocent bystanders. If you are leaving the water for any length of time, carry your equipment to a spot that is sheltered from the wind. However, if you want to leave board and rig by the water's edge ready for the next foray, make sure they are connected, have the mast pointing downwind and lay the board on top.

If you are leaving the board on its own, have its nose pointing into wind and fin facing up. However, this is risky for any length of time. The wind direction might change and just a light breeze can be enough to send the board cartwheeling down the beach.

As for the sail – the simple rule is never to leave a rigged rig unattended, even in the lightest of winds. You can point the mast tip into wind and weigh it down with sand or stones, or tie it to a post with the uphaul rope. However, if the wind is swirling and unpredictable, you should either attach it to the board and leave it as shown (see page 59), or better still, de-rig it.

Rights of Way

As a beginner with not much speed and even less manoeuvrability, the best thing is to keep out of everyone's way. If you so much as sniff a potential collision, drop the rig and sit on the board until the danger has passed.

However, as you practise and improve, you are likely to find yourself on crowded weekend waters and you'll also start going faster, at which point the duty falls on you to learn the primary rules of the road.

For sail-powered craft, there is a long and detailed maritime highway code, but in the early stages of recreational windsurfing there are just three rules to be aware of that cover the majority of potential confrontations. Unfortunately, these are difficult to explain without excavating a little more nautical jargon.

The Head-On Situation

Where two boards are sailing across the wind towards each other, the one with the wind blowing from the right has right of

Windsurfers like to stick together. The best spots can get pretty crowded so it is just as well to know the rules of the road. (John Carter)

way and the other must take avoiding action.

The easiest way to work it out is to look at your hands. If your front hand is the right hand, then the wind is from the right and you have right of way. If your front hand is the left hand, you need to be ready to move.

This is commonly known as the 'port starboard rule'. Port is left and starboard is right when you face the front of the board. If you have the wind coming from the right, you are said to be on 'starboard tack' and have rights over a board on 'port tack'. As the boards get close, the one on starboard tack can shout 'starboard' to let the other know that he should steer off.

Upwind, Downwind

When two boards are converging but have the wind on the same side, the upwind board must steer clear. This is logical. The downwind sailor will have his back to the situation and so may not be aware of the other's presence. Also, if the boards get close, the upwind one will leave the other in a wind shadow, taking away his power and ability to steer.

Two more terms for you – 'windward' signifies upwind and 'leeward' downwind. The windward board gives way to the leeward board.

Overtaking

Away from the racecourse (where the rules on overtaking get incredibly complicated), the accepted rule is that the overtaking board keeps clear. At the same time, the overtaken must hold its line and not do anything rash (like a sudden swerve upwind) that might stop the other keeping clear.

The Reality

These rules were originally written for yachts and dinghies, which travel slower and are generally piloted by folk who know the rules. They not only know what to do but have more time in which to consider their actions. This is not to say that all windsurfers are lawless hooligans, but things happen so much faster that impact may have occurred before anyone has had a chance to decide who should have done what.

Keep the above rules in mind but tem-

per them with a lot of common sense. Make your intentions clear early. Head-on confrontations can turn into a game of involuntary 'chicken', where both hold their line, thinking the other will steer, until the last moment when both steer away – but, sadly, in the same direction. So in all situations, make a bold move early and stick to it. If you are unsure which way to go, head up into wind, then at least you will slow down.

Most collisions take place when someone spontaneously goes into a turn without looking. So before you change direction, look ahead, behind, upwind and downwind. This is a message that will be strongly reinforced when we discuss the planing manoeuvres.

When windsurfers fall, there is not much to see. The rig lies flat to the water and a small wave can hide the head from view. So if you have fallen, make yourself visible by waving your hands around and getting back on your board as quickly as possible. If you are sailing and you see someone fall in the distance, note their position and just keep your eyes on the road ahead.

Your Fellow Water Users

Motor-powered craft give way to sailing craft but this does not include commercial shipping. A super tanker, which has a turning radius of 10km, cannot keep out of the way of windsurfers or any other pleasure craft for that matter. The fact is that you should not be in a shipping lane in the first place.

Usually the motor versus sail conflict is irrelevant. Areas that are popular with powerboats are not usually that good for windsurfing and vice versa. But if you go out in an area populated by all sorts, give everything a wide berth.

I will look at more specific rules, notably how to behave in breaking surf, later in the book (see page 154).

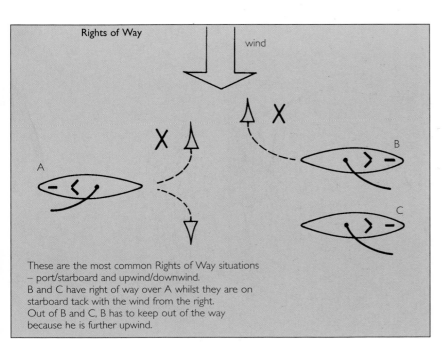

Rights of Way

wind

A

X

X

B

C

These are the most common Rights of Way situations – port/starboard and upwind/downwind.
B and C have right of way over A whilst they are on starboard tack with the wind from the right.
Out of B and C, B has to keep out of the way because he is further upwind.

CHAPTER 5

THE HARNESS AND FOOTSTRAPS

Both the harness and footstraps were conceived to increase your control and enjoyment in strong winds. It was thought only logical, therefore, that you should at least be able to plane before attempting to use them. Which was fine, except that the likelihood of the right strength of wind coinciding with precious days off tended to be so remote that it was often years before you finally amassed enough experience.

Today, they can be introduced much earlier. Thanks to modern designs, you can start to gather the necessary skills in whatever weather prevails. By using the forward 'training' positions, you can get used to the footstraps in very light winds. You can also practise with the harness in winds as light as 3–6kt (force 2).

When stronger winds arrive, you just use the same basic skills to resist a little more power, go faster and pop on to the plane. So it is that planing, the official windsurfing drug, is now achievable within weeks rather than years. However, there is such a thing as too soon.

THE RIGHT TIME

After your first course there has to be a period of putting some water miles behind you. Given favourable conditions, progress at this stage is likely to be meteoric. What you really notice is just how much more comfortable you become with the environment, the equipment – the whole feeling. The unknown is now familiar. That initial anxiety evaporates and you find yourself mentally liberated to 'go for it', as the coaches love to say.

The very last thing you need at this stage is to burst that confidence bubble by tying yourself to the rig with a harness line.

If you start in the harness before your rig control is up to scratch, you are likely to suffer a few falls still attached to the boom. Although not dangerous in a light wind, it is nevertheless a little unnerving. If you are at all nervous about using the harness, you will develop a tense, defensive stance that is sure to be counter-productive.

There is no 'right' time to try the harness. It might be a week; it might be a year. The only criteria are your stance and rig control. These are the stages you need to go through before trying to hook in.

A Bigger Sail
The moment you feel comfortable and understand the mechanics of steering and turning, take out a bigger rig. The extra power immediately reduces the room for error. You have no choice. Either you hold the mast upright, face the pull and use

Taking out a bigger rig, in this case a 5.5sq m, in a 7–10kt (force 3) wind, makes you develop your stance and rig control. When you find yourself instinctively extending away from the rig and moving back down the board for more leverage, you know that you are ready for the harness and footstraps. (John Carter)

The harness opens the door to strong winds and hours of harmless posing. (Dave White)

your body as a counterbalance, or you get pulled over. For the very first sessions, an adult weighing about 72kg (158lb) would start with a sail around 4.5sq m. For this next step, you should move up to a sail of around 5.5sq m assuming a wind speed of 1–10kt (force 1–3).

Feel the Power Point

A bigger sail heightens your sensitivity to where the sail is pulling from. If you relax your arms, you may feel that one of them has to work harder than the other. If so, move your hands up or down the boom until you feel the load is shared equally between them. If the back hand is taking more pressure, then slide both hands back on the boom and vice versa if the front hand is over-working.

The next exercise is to try sailing with the hands closer and closer together. If you get to the point where both hands are touching or where you can even let one hand go, then you have found the boom's balance point. Finding, feeling and understanding this balance point is crucial to setting up the harness lines and using the harness.

Trim the Board

'Trimming' describes the act of making the smallest adjustments so the board moves through the water with the minimum resistance. As the board picks up speed, you need to become more sensitive to its movement. Is it gliding on the surface or grinding and slapping noisily into every wavelet?

The aim is to make it ride flat and level both on the lateral and longitudinal planes.

Obviously, moving the feet and body forward or back will make the nose or tail either lift or sink, but it is actually more subtle that that.

Experiment with heel and toe pressure. When you are off the plane using a daggerboard or central fin, the board often rides more smoothly if it is slightly banked over so the leeward edge is engaged. You achieve this by putting the back foot across the centreline and by pressing on the toes.

Try to direct the power of the sail directly against the board's balance point. Off the plane, this point is going to be level with the daggerboard or central fin. You can find it by bringing your feet closer and closer together until you can stand on one leg without making the board turn.

Trying to sail on one leg and/or with one hand makes you sensitive to the balance points of both the board and rig. (John Carter)

You can feel the board drag through the water if you sink the upwind edge. Use toe pressure to level it out – the improvement is instant. (John Carter)

Stance

A more powerful sail can help you eliminate some bad habits – and take on some new ones. While the fundamentals of stance remain the same, be aware of certain points:

- Relax the fingers. A bizarre instinct tells us to squeeze the boom as the force increases. Actually, the strongest and least tiring grip is to make a hook out of the fingers and thumb and just drape them over the top.
- Extend the arms. See how long you can hang on to heavy suitcases with the arms bent – it is the same when windsurfing. If you bend the arms, the relatively weak forearms and biceps have to bear most of the weight. If you extend them, much of the load is transferred to the stronger back muscles.
- Shoulders. Adjusting the angle of the rig is now done by keeping the arms extended and by pushing and pulling from the shoulders.
- Upper body. To gain the best leverage over the rig as it pulls harder, think of imitating the shape of the figure seven – arms extended and parallel with the water, shoulders outboard, hips lifted and forward and the whole body quite straight.

- Feet and legs. You may be going faster but resist the temptation to spread your legs as a way to render yourself an immovable object. You may feel more stable but you will also be less agile and sensitive to the board. Keep the feet shoulder-width apart and point the toes diagonally in towards the sail so everything is facing the power.

Last but not least – keep your head up and look where you're going!

THE HARNESS

When I started windsurfing, the harness had yet to be invented. And whilst I look back on those pioneering years with a warm glow, no amount of nostalgia can erase the memory of the pain of trying to hang on to that boom in strong winds. Desperate for relief, we would constantly change grip, hook our elbows over the boom, do anything to try and relieve our burning forearms. Back on land, our arm muscles were so shot away that we could barely raise a pint glass.

So when the harness arrived on the scene, the magnitude and immediacy of the change it made to our sport can have been no less startling than when early alpine skiers were offered their first ski lift. With the weight of our bodies taking the strain, we could stay out in strong winds all day. We had more time to practise and, no longer consumed by the physical challenge, we could devote our energies to working on new skills and manoeuvres.

Today, people experiment with a harness as soon as they achieve the most basic rig control in moderate winds. There is no need for it to be windy, a big sail is not required, and you don't have to be planing.

Initially, the main aims are to get the feeling of taking some of the rig's load on the body and to learn to control the power through the hips. If you persevere for a long time without a harness, you get used to controlling the power primarily via a push-pull action of the arms. In a harness you are attached to the rig via a loop of rope to the hips. Although you can still use the arms to a certain extent, it is through moving the hips that you balance the rig.

Choosing and Fitting the Harness

Life in the harness begins with a fitting session. The two most widely used designs are the waist and the seat harness. The waist harness fastens around the waist like a wide belt. The seat harness is a little more substantial. You step into it through leg straps and it fits right around your backside, hence its other rather unflattering tag of 'nappy' harness.

There are pros and cons to each. The seat offers more support but the leg straps do restrict your movement. The waist harness may ride up and be less comfortable if you are holding down a lot of power but it is light, easy to get on and off and doesn't get in the way. It also has a marginally higher hook, which makes hooking in and out easier.

The waist design, originally just worn by wave sailors, has become increasingly popular with all grades of windsurfer, including beginners. But the choice has to be yours. The waist harness does not suit everybody, particularly the more portly – if you have no discernible waist, then it won't stay put and will ride up to your chest as soon as you hook in. Others find a waist harness uncomfortable around the ribs. The answer is to try on as many as possible. A good shop will have a rope for you to hook into and hang your weight against. Swing around for a while and see if it spreads the load evenly or just shifts around and gives you pressure points.

In most designs, the spreader bar and hook lie more or less over the navel. It has to be tight or the hook will flop around, making hooking in, and particularly hooking out, a lot harder. With the seat harness, tighten the leg straps first as they stop the harness riding up.

When wet, the webbing straps can stretch a little, especially new ones. So after ten minutes or so of sailing, you may have to come in and tighten everything up.

Other Features

On the front of the harness sits the hook and spreader bar. The hook is 'V' shaped to prevent the line knotting round it; the spreader is designed to divert the load to the back of the harness and stop it tightening around the ribs.

Other essential features are the quick-release buckles and straps, which allow you to get out of the harness immediately in the very rare event that you should fall with the hook snagged.

Whichever model you end up buying, practise getting out, as well as getting into it, before you go on the water.

Harness Lines

The harness lines are made from rope covered in a sheath of hard plastic, which not only protects the rope from chaffing but also makes it hang in an even loop. Each end of the line attaches to the boom through an array of crafty means. Some simply slide through the arms of the boom, requiring that you take the back of the boom off first. Others, more conveniently, use a buckle and Velcro.

The length of the line depends on your size, length of arm and the type of sailing you are doing. The time-honoured way of measuring the line is to put your elbow in the loop and see where the boom reaches on your forearm. A popular starting length is where the boom reaches the top of the wrist, which is long enough to give you a little freedom around the hips but not so long that the line keeps dropping out by mistake. Harness lines are traditionally measured in inches, ranging from about 18–30in to accommodate the tallest and shortest folk and their different styles of sailing. For example, wave sailors and freestylers like very long harness lines; racers tend to like them very short. I hesitate to generalize as it is such a personal thing but 22–26in is the range within which most people fall.

Some lines give you about 4in of adjustment – a nice feature if you are at the experimental stage or sharing your rig with a taller/shorter person. Those with a buckle system can even be adjusted while you are hooked in and sailing.

Setting Up the Lines

The harness links your hips, which are your

The seat harness on the right offers more support but the waist harness on the left allows more freedom of movement and is easier to use. (John Carter)

The harness must spread the load evenly. Test it by hooking into a line on the beach. If it rides up, squashes your ribs, or gives you pressure points, hand it back. (John Carter)

centre of gravity, to the power point of the sail. In order that you pull directly against the power, the end of the loop must line up with the power point of the sail.

To set up the lines on the beach, all you have to do is find the balance point of the boom (which corresponds to the power point in the sail) and then attach the ends of the line either side of it.

In a moderate wind, support the rig on the beach and shuffle your hands together until you can balance the rig with them touching. Where the hands touch is the boom's balance point. Now attach the line with each end equidistant from that balance point, about 20cm (8in) apart. Do the same on the other side of the boom.

So is that it? Well, it will do for practice in light wind but the harness lines will need adjusting as the wind strengthens. Their length and positioning is a never-ending conundrum for windsurfers as they change equipment, tweak the rig settings, try different disciplines and develop their own style and preferences.

Hooking In and Out

The biggest enemy to the debutante harness user is a gusty wind. As you try to get used to the already strange feeling of being at one with the boom, the last thing you need are unexpected surges and lulls heaving you off balance or dropping you in backwards.

If you can find a clear stretch of beach or bank open to steady winds of 3–10kt (force 2–3), the best place to train is on dry land. Taking away the balance variable allows you to concentrate on the job in hand.

Lay the board across the wind, take the fin out or dig it in the sand and drop into your sailing stance.

There is a very simple principle to hooking in and out, which you discover the second after you've been pulled on your face for the first time. Let me save you the trouble – to hook in, pull the rig towards you, on no account move towards the rig.

To get the hook to drop on to the line, keep your weight committed to wind-

To measure the length, put your elbow in the loop. The boom should come up to about the top of your wrist.

To set the lines, move the hands closer together until you can hold the rig with one hand. This is the boom's balance point. Place the ends of the harness line equidistant from that point (about 20cm/8in apart).

Setting up the Harness Sequence *(John Carter and Dave White)*

If you've got it right, your centre of gravity will pull directly against the power of the sail and you will be able to balance the rig (momentarily at least) using the body alone.

ward, pull the rig towards you and with a gentle push of the hips and a bend of the knees, drop the hook on to the line. Then drop the hips away from the boom to take the load on the harness. I'm sure this is self-evident but I think I should remind you that if, by contrast, you decide to move your body inboard towards the rig, as soon as tension comes on the line, you will get pulled over.

In any situation where tension comes off the line, it will drop out of the hook. Most people hook out by pulling the rig sharply towards them, but you can also do it by taking the pressure on the arms and pushing the hips forward.

The First Water Session

The first session is entirely devoted to the practice of hooking in and out and learning to trust in the harness. To begin with, what is supposed to be an energy-saving device will leave you a crumpled, sweating mass. The arms, so used to taking the strain and trimming the sail, refuse to relinquish the task and hang on harder than normal.

> **TOP TIP**
> *Imagine that the boom is a piano. As soon as you hook into the harness, start tinkling the imaginary ivories with the lightest fingers as a way of forcing yourself to relinquish your grip on the boom, relax the arms and take the load on the harness.*

With every run, try to loosen your grip and push the hips away from the boom. You should feel more and more of the load go through the harness until your hands are just draped over the boom.

The proof that the harness is indeed taking the load is to let one hand go altogether. By dropping one or even both arms, you are forced to control the power with the body alone.

Power Control in the Harness

It is unrealistic to think that once you have mastered the harness, your arms will become redundant and can hang limply by your sides. The truth is that the arms and hips work together. The hips make the major balance changes, whilst the hands, resting lightly on the boom, make the minor adjustments to the sail angle.

There are two ways to control the power in the harness, the first is by moving the hips towards or away from the boom and the second is by sheeting in and out. When hooked in, your hips and bottom are like a pendulum, able to swing in and out or forward and back. Standing upright in your normal stance, you look upwind and see a gust coming across the water. As you feel it in the sail, drop the hips further outboard, away from the boom. When the wind drops, lift the hips towards the boom. It is just a case of moving your ballast towards and away from the sail to balance the power of the wind but without moving the rig.

Although your movement is slightly restricted, you can still change the angle of the sail when hooked in. To open the sail and sheet out, come inboard over the centreline, push the back hand away, at the same time twisting the hips towards the nose. To sheet in, pull in the back

The key to hooking in is to keep your weight committed against the rig with your weight on your heels. Pull the boom towards you while at the same easing the hips forwards to drop the hook on to the line. (Dave White)

To take the load on the harness, extend the arms and drop the hips back. (Dave White)

If you lean forward to engage the line, there is only one place you'll end up. (Dave White)

It looks like shameless posing, but dropping a hand off the boom is the best way to make yourself commit your weight to the harness. (John Carter)

hand, at the same time twisting the hips back in towards the sail and dropping them outboard to resist the power. Basically the hips rotate in order to stay parallel to the boom as it opens and closes.

FOOTSTRAPS

When the early windsurfers led their boards to the open seas, they soon discovered that a little speed and a small wave made a devastating combination. However, the thrill of take-off and momentary flight soon gave way to the frustration caused by man and equipment parting company. The problem was at least partly solved by the addition of footstraps or 'toe loops' as they were first called. Wedged under the footstraps, the feet not only stayed attached to the board as it left the water but they could also be used to control its trajectory.

Whether or not you decide to take to the air, footstraps are indispensable if you are to remain attached to your board in strong winds. (John Carter)

Positions	Front strap just behind the mastfoot, back strap just behind the daggerboard.	Positions	Front straps behind the daggerboard, half-way between the centreline and rail. Back straps equidistant from the rail and about 15cm (6in) in front of the fin.
Wind	3–10kt (force 2–3) non-planing to marginal planing.	Wind	7–16kt (force 3–4). Marginal planing to planing.
Set-up	With or without daggerboard or central fin.	Set-up	Without daggerboard. Needs to be fitted with a big fin, at least 38cm (15in).
For whom?	A first time strap user who is reasonably happy using the harness in moderate winds.	For whom?	First- or second-time strap user with fair rig and power control.
For what?	Getting used to sailing with the feet fixed with a reasonable pull in the sail.	For what?	To experience the sensation of fully planing, footsteering and carve gybing for the first time.

Positions   Right out there on the rail.
Wind   7–21kt (force 3–5), fully planing conditions.
Set-up   Without daggerboard. Fully powered with a big fin.
For whom?   A proficient planing sailor looking to hold down a big sail and crank it up to full speed on all points of sailing.
For what?   Taking up the position to resist the lift from a big fin. Cruising and ultimately racing.

These are the ideal positions for first-time training straps in that although you can sail in them off the plane, you need a reasonable pull in the sail to make it comfortable. They are just far enough back to allow the nose to rise and for you to feel the first stages of planing.

This is the real thing. Unless you are a flyweight, these straps cannot be used off the plane in a normal stance (you can use any straps off the plane if you lean forward enough on the boom). The straps are more outboard, which means that you are expected to go fast enough to get some lift off the fin and then move the feet outboard to avoid capsizing.

As well as being the best position from which to learn to footsteer and eventually carve gybe, this is the best all-round strap position for training and having fun.

So long as you are not over-powered, you are sufficiently far back and outboard to plane fully and comfortably.

The straps are not so far outboard that you have to display super-delicate trim getting into them. There is plenty of room for error so they are still good for the first-time effort.

This is where our sober, benign, entry-level platform tries to turn itself into a Formula race board. You are no longer in training mode. The straps are placed right out on the edge so you can resist the lift of a large fin, which has to be balanced by a big sail (at least 7.5sq m for an average adult) in a wind of 11–16kt (force 4). This is when you not only find yourself planing in marginal breezes but also able to smoke upwind, downwind and everything in between.

As for gybing, once you have set yourself up for speed with the straps outboard, manoeuvring becomes more of a function than a joy. To 'carve' (bank the board over so that it 'carves' around on its inside edge) from this stance, the feet end up uncomfortably far apart. The carve gybe, even when learning, is easier on a narrower board or at least one where the straps are more centrally mounted.

Footstrap Positions *(John Carter)*

Footstraps soon became an indispensable accessory on any board that was designed to plane (which, these days, is all of them). They keep your feet anchored in the face of driving gusts and sluicing waves, offering another level of control even in less-threatening conditions. At speed they allow you to wear the board like a shoe. For example, if it is lifting off the water, you can just curl the foot up in the strap and pull it down.

Footstrap Positions

The latest entry-level boards offer a bewildering choice of footstrap positions designed to coincide with every step of your progress.

As you learn to handle more power and ease on to the plane, two things happen:

1. You instinctively stand further and further back on the board to get better leverage over the rig and to allow the nose to lift and the board to plane on its tail.
2. As the fin accelerates through the water, it tries to find its way to the surface, literally tipping the board over. Therefore, you need to stand more outboard on the windward edge to balance that lift.

Most boards come with either three or four straps – two at the front and either one or two at the back, depending on the width of the tail. The board illustrated opposite is actually offering three sets of positions. There is a rough guide to the advantages of each.

The Spread

With each of the above combinations, there is a choice of screw holes for each side of both the front and back straps so you can alter the distance between them. The distance between your feet when you stand determines both your stability and manoeuvrability. With the feet close together, the centre of gravity is high and the base is narrow, which makes you easy to knock over. If they are wide apart, you have a stable base and a low centre of gravity but your stance will be static and wooden.

Ideally, the feet should be roughly shoulder-width apart so you are stable but can still shift your weight easily from one foot to the other. This is the same stance as a tennis player takes up ready to receive a serve or a wrestler sparring for position.

The Fit

The footstraps themselves may be adjusted using a simple Velcro fastening system. For them to be of any use, they have to accommodate the whole foot, so you can curl your toes up and grip the strap in a moment of need. Adjust them to fit tightly across the widest part of the foot. There must be no gap between the foot and the top of the strap and you should be able to see all your toes poking through (unless covered by a shoe, of course).

Understandably, people harbour dark thoughts of falling and getting their feet trapped. As a precautionary measure, they make the footstraps so ridiculously small that the little toe barely fits through. If you adjust them as suggested, the feet will always slip out when you drop past that point of no return. On the other hand, making them too small is generally the reason why people struggle to trim and

Velcro makes the footstraps easy to adjust. (John Carter)

The straps fit tightly across the widest part of the foot and the feet are deep enough in so that all your toes are right through and can curl up to grip them. (John Carter)

control the board from the straps, especially on small boards. Ultimately, the deeper you put your feet in the straps, the greater your control, especially in the air and through the manoeuvres.

Which Straps to Mount?

How you approach your first attempt at footstraps will depend on the wind, the level of your harness work and your ambition.

Rather than taking a stab in the dark, one tactic is to go out on a bare, strapless board with as big a sail as you can comfortably handle. Note how far back you can stand comfortably when up to full speed in gusts of wind. Return to shore and screw in the straps nearest to those positions.

Using the Training Straps

Training straps help you to use footstraps a lot earlier in your windsurfing career. The case for mounting them is that you are then able to practise in non-planing conditions and get used to balancing without moving the feet. At full planing speed, moving the feet, especially on a small board, will invite an explosive change of trim.

Stability, the advantage of a big wide board, is also its downfall because it allows you to stagger around without getting a rap on your knuckles. Putting your feet in the straps, even in a light wind, is good discipline in that you have to keep the feet still.

Balancing without moving the feet comes from anticipating changes and moving just the core of the body – the hips and bottom.

Next time you are standing on a crowded bus, try keeping your balance without holding on or moving your feet as it starts, stops, and goes round bends. To begin with, you may lurch around, irritating your fellow travellers; but you will very quickly learn to relax, keepi the head and shoulders still and flex the knees and ankles as a way to shift your centre of gravity. It is much the same with your feet in the straps.

The Art of Stepping In

The next thing that people usually want to

know is how to step back on the board without sinking the tail.

The wide boards have enough volume in the tail to allow you to move back into the forward training straps without causing an upset. Beyond that, you need to become aware of a couple of new principles, which are explained in more detail in Chapter 7.

In the same way as a water-ski, the board lifts out of the water as it accelerates and so effectively becomes more buoyant. To sail the board from the tail, speed is essential. You also balance the board using the rig. Every move you make with the body, you make an opposite move with the rig – as you move back, therefore, you hold the rig forward. The

weight and power going down through the mastfoot then holds the nose down.

When putting your feet in the straps, be strict with yourself from the start about doing it in the correct order.

1. With the board across the wind, stand with the feet just in front of their respective straps and hook into the harness.
2. Bear away a few degrees off the wind. Bend the knees to take more weight in the harness, lift the front foot and slide it gently into its strap. Hold the rig forward.
3. Lift the back foot towards its strap. Feel for it with the toes and then gradually transfer weight on to it.

Get into good habits from day one and learn to move your feet without upsetting the trim of the board. To succeed, you must stay on your toes and move your feet without causing a sudden shift of weight. (John Carter)

Sailing in training straps in winds of 3–10kt (force 2–3). The board is not planing yet but you are getting used to standing further back and balancing without moving your feet. (John Carter)

Remember the sequence – hook in, front foot in strap, back foot in strap. This routine will serve you for all strengths of wind and sizes of board.

Warning!

The hardest part about using straps on a nervous board in a planing wind is stepping back on the board and sliding the feet in without upsetting the trim. When the straps are right forward on a big board, you can clamber into them with all the subtlety of a young elephant and get away with it. In other words, the training footstraps can make you lazy. So keep putting the bar up. Once you are comfortable in the forward set and beginning to make the board plane, move the straps further and further back until you are sailing the board right from the tail, as the designer intended.

PLANING

I will never forget the first time I made a small windsurfer plane. I had borrowed one of the first 'sinkers', as they were then called (a board that would sink under your weight unless it was moving). After many minutes going nowhere I was hit by a gust, stepped back towards the straps and suddenly felt as if I had been shot from a canon. Having done 0–60mph in about three seconds, I looked down to see that only the tail of the board was in contact with the water. I was flying. I felt as if the turbocharger had kicked in and someone had stolen both the steering wheel and the brake, leaving me teetering on an emotional knife edge between exhilaration

When you plane, the board overtakes its own bow wave, lifts out of the water and skims on the back area behind the footstraps. Sheer joy! (John Carter)

and terror. However, after a couple of runs I vowed never to bother with light winds again. I had been injected with the planing drug for which an antidote has yet to be found.

What is Happening

At slow speeds, a board sits deep in the water and pushes through it like a boat producing a large bow wave. As you sheet in the sail, it rises, overtakes its own bow wave and skims along on the top of it. It no longer displaces water but rides right on the surface. Only the back third of the board, the area behind the straps, makes contact. The water suddenly seems to offer no resistance. There is a feeling of weightlessness and efficiency as you begin to travel as quickly as a powerful speed-boat, except that the windsurfer mnages it with less noise and stink.

Planing Conditions

The biggest, widest racing boards, which accommodate the giant rigs, will plane in as little as 7kt of wind (barely a force 3), whilst the smallest wave board may require winds of 17–21kt (force 5) or more, depending on the size and skill of its rider.

As a beginner, the rig should not be much bigger than 6.5sq m, so even on a large board you will need a wind of at least 11kt (the bottom end of a force 4) to push you on to the plane.

The smallest and biggest boards actually need about the same amount of wind to keep them on the plane. However, because the smaller ones start semi-submerged, they create a lot of drag initially and so need more wind and power to drive them to the surface, which is why one of the most treasured windsurfing skills is early planing technique. Through delicate sail and board trim and energetic 'pumping' of the sail to create an artificial gust of wind, experienced windsurfers can get the smallest boards planing in remarkably little wind. Early planing techniques are discussed in Chapter 7.

Planing Characteristics

The smaller the board, the more sudden the transition to planing. Off the plane, a small board will be moving at about

3–8kph (2–5mph). But when it releases on to the plane, it will immediately accelerate to at least 24kph (15mph).

By contrast, a big, and more importantly, wide board sits much higher in the water and therefore makes a gentler

A bigger sail (6.5sq m) and a wind speed of 11–16kt (force 4) provide the potential to plane. It is the same board as before but the footstraps have been moved back and outboard so you can sail it from the tail and resist the lift from the fin. Committed to the harness to power the rig, bear off and as the power increases, lift the front foot under you and into the strap.

Getting into Straps Sequence *(John Carter)*

By holding the rig forward, the power holds the nose down as you move back. The back foot stays across the centreline so it can hold the board level as the front foot moves to the edge. Above all, you must provide a constant source of power to drive you on to the plane by staying sheeted in and keeping the rig still.

Wind Direction

In these moderate conditions, there is no hurry to move the back foot in. As the board accelerates, you will feel the fin beginning to lift the windward edge. Gradually move the foot back and outboard until it rests against the strap.

Shift the weight on to the front foot while at the same time tilting the rig back slightly to avoid being pulled off balance. Without looking down, find the entrance to the strap, stay on your toes, and be sure not to make any sudden weight shift on to the back foot.

Wind Direction

Slide the foot all the way into the strap and gradually ease more weight on to it. Keep the board riding level and only drop weight on to the heels as you feel the windward edge lifting.

transition to planing. At around 11kph (7mph), it will begin to lift and ride on less surface area. In this 'marginal' or semi-planing state, you can move back into the straps from where the board will release fully on to the plane if you have enough power.

This ability of the new wide boards to plane at slow speeds is of most benefit to the improver. The whole sensation is introduced gradually, allowing him to develop the appropriate responses and techniques in a state of excitement, rather than blind panic.

Accelerating on to the Plane

On a big board, the difference between non-planing and planing is simply that you have more power in the form of a stronger wind or a bigger sail. To a certain extent, it is just a case of committing to the harness and transferring that extra power through the feet and into the board. There are, however, a few other things to think about.

- **Bear away**. The sail produces more power if the board is heading downwind than if it is pointing upwind. As you bear away (about 15 degrees downwind of a beam reach), the wind blows from behind and drives you forward. You need a lot more wind to plane if you stay on a close reach.
- **Rig forward**. Remember the key point of holding the rig away on extended arms is so the mast is vertical. When the rig is forward, it holds the nose down and the board stays level. If you pull it back, its weight is liable to sink the tail, which is like throwing out an anchor.

- **Step back**. When the pull in the sail increases, your natural reaction should be to step back to distance yourself from the mastfoot and gain more leverage. As you take the pressure off the front foot and move it back towards its strap, you allow the nose to rise and the board to lift on to its planing surface and accelerate.
- **Feet placement**. The order of events for planing is just the same as for non-planing conditions – hook in, front foot in strap, back foot in strap.

This all too common result of trying to move into the straps, sinking the tail and heading up into the wind, is primarily the result of not bearing away enough and stamping into the straps with heavy feet. (John Carter)

Sailing on the Plane

Now that everything is happening so much more quickly, like all good sportsmen, you need to adopt an attitude of calm urgency – relaxed yet poised to react. Because less of the board is in contact with the water when you are planing, it is a lot more sensitive to pressure from the feet and the sail. To keep it tracking smoothly over the water, you have to deliver a constant source of power. Make all adjustments as subtle as possible. The bigger the movement of feet or rig, the more violently the board will react.

Offence not Defence

In a planing wind, there is a considerable pull in the sail when you sheet in. The key is to resist but not fight it. For the first few runs, your body will flood with foreign chemicals and nothing will stop you 'digging in' to stop yourself from being lifted off your feet and dumped unceremoniously in the water. But as you become more comfortable with the situation, start to view the enemy as a friend. The rig wants to pull you along, so let it. Your plight is similar to that of inexperienced waterskiers. To begin with, they pull on the rope as if trying to arrest the boat in its tracks and heave it back to shore. It is only when they give in to the boat and allow themselves to be pulled along that everything falls into place. Effectively the rig is your speedboat – try and go with the force that is pulling you along.

It is so important to understand that, within reason, speed is your friend. As you accelerate, the power in the rig softens and the board rides more smoothly over the water. Consider how much easier it is to balance and turn a bicycle if you let it run. Likewise, a windsurfer is more comfortable and controllable when it is fully on the plane.

Harness Techniques

With the rig generating more power, the whole success of this next stage hinges on you taking and controlling that power through the harness. Many achieve this by sitting down in the harness. While this works, it is a defensive, passive reaction, which encourages you to lean too far back and often leads to bad board trim. A good

windsurfer lowers his weight to resist the initial surge but then stands up in the harness to un-weight the board. Rather than just digging-in and dropping on to the heels, he drives the board along with taught legs, using the whole foot to trim the board; coming up on to the toes in a lull, rocking back on to the heels in a gust. It is a more natural and more comfortable posture that leaves you in the best position to move. The power point of the sail is about eye height. The feeling you want is that of pulling directly against it.

When the waves start to build and the power increases to the point where you begin to feel slightly vulnerable, then you can bend your legs a little more to lower your centre of gravity but the rest of your posture stays the same.

Constant Flow

The board needs a constant source of power to get it on the plane and keep it there. If you constantly power up and de-power the rig, you will lurch on and off the plane like a learner driver 'kangarooing' his way down the street.

Obviously, a constant wind helps but even if it is gusty, try to predict the changes. Hold the hips and shoulders as still as possible to keep a steady tension through the harness line. When a gust arrives, drive against it gradually so the board accelerates smoothly rather than being jolted by a sudden pulse of power.

Hanging off the Rig

As you accelerate, compensate for the fact that you are moving back over the tail by suspending yourself in the harness so some of your weight is diverted via the boom into the foot of the mast. Once the board is fully planing and the fin is lifting, you can stand up again and transfer more weight back to your feet. This whole concept of hanging off the boom and sharing the power between your feet and the mastfoot becomes increasingly important as you move to shorter boards.

Gusts and Lulls on the Plane

When you run into a lull on the plane, the power going through the rig and into the mastfoot will decrease and the board will begin to ride tail heavy. Your first reaction

must be to compensate by staying hooked in, hanging down off the boom and swinging your hips forward towards the nose. By so doing, you take some of the weight off your feet, direct it through the rig into the mastfoot, and push the nose down. At this level, the hips balance the board and rig by moving through 360 degrees – in and out, forward and back.

Lack of anticipation leads to the most frequent blunder, which is getting trapped in the footstraps as the wind dies. Feel when the board is starting to drag through the water and get into the habit of moving forward of the straps before it drops completely off the plane.

> **TOP TIP**
> To get your body moving in the right direction, try sailing in the performance straps in a light wind. The only way to do it without sinking the tail is to lean right forward, which is uncomfortable but effective.

Steering on the Plane

This is very straightforward – to turn left, press on the left edge; to turn right, press on the right edge. When you are on the plane, you steer with the feet. The rig is now just the motor pulling you along. You are surfing, moving your body from one edge to the other to bank the board over and turn it along its inside edge. Welcome to carving. It is as simple as it sounds and one of the great windsurfing sensations where the board literally gouges an arc through the water.

Turning Upwind

Take the back foot out and place it just forward of the strap with the heel over the upwind edge. Rock back on both heels to pressure the upwind edge and you will carve upwind. How quickly you turn depends on how much you pressure the edge and how steeply you bank the board.

Turning Downwind

This time, place the back foot on the downwind side of the board. Let the body come over the centreline then flex the ankles and knees in towards the sail, and pressure the toes of the back foot to press in the downwind edge. The board will turn

On the plane, the feet take over the steering duties and bank the board over to make it turn. By easing the weight on to the heels to sink the windward edge, the board carves along that edge and turns upwind. (John Carter)

downwind and accelerate as you do so.

In the upwind carve, you can use both feet to pressure the edge. In the downwind turn, the front foot, on a wide board at least, is on the wrong side so the back foot applies most of the pressure.

In both cases, the board will continue to carve until it drops off the plane, reaches dead upwind or dead downwind, or you level it off.

The skill of foot steering and carving the board is fundamental to so much of what happens at a more advanced stage. Whether you are riding a 12m (40ft) wave or just turning round on the plane in an 11–16kt (force 4) wind, the basic skill of holding an edge is the same.

As soon as you feel comfortable and in control on the plane, start to experiment with edge pressure. Sail across the wind and then try to steer an 'S' course upwind and downwind like a slalom skier. These are the stages to go through:

1. Make gentle curves by moving the back foot from the upwind edge to the downwind edge and pressing gently.
2. As you gain confidence, bank the board more and more steeply to make sharper curves. Use the hips to lead the whole body from one side to the other so you can commit more of your weight to the edges.
3. As you change direction, you have to alter the angle of the sail to keep it powered up. Sheet in as you carve upwind, sheet out as you carve downwind. Be sure to hold the rig forward and away from you by extending the front arm.

Warning!

Beware of the seductive thrills of just blasting along on the plane! It's fun, it's exhilarating and you learn to relax into the harness and cope with the changing wind and undulating water. However, long reaches also breed sloth and immobility. Improving from this stage and making the quantum leap towards carving turns is all about dynamic movement.

CHAPTER 6

THE WATERSTART

To date, this book has unfolded a bit like a 1940s love film. Soft focus and careful editing leave us with a sugar-sweet story devoid of the brutalities of everyday life. In the last chapter for example, I glibly suggested that in order to get planing, you wait for more wind or take out a bigger sail and commit more of your weight against the sail. This is true enough but assumes you managed to get going in the first place.

Pulling the rig out of the water, for many, is windsurfing's most laborious and demoralizing task. Worse still, you are now being asked to hoist a bigger and therefore heavier rig in a strengthening wind, which will do its best to drive it back down again, whilst at the same time making the water rougher and the board less stable. During those first planing sessions, 90 per cent of your time, energy and patience may be taken up trying to heave the rig into life, and just 10 per cent actually sailing along … until you learn to waterstart.

Rather than climb on the board, you swim to the rig, release it from the water, and manoeuvre it in such a way that it lifts

As well as being a far easier and less tiring way to get going in planing winds, the waterstart opens the door to smaller boards. (John Carter)

you on to the board. In most instances, this is a far more efficient way of getting going in strong winds because the wind is doing the work. You are going with the force rather than having to fight it. Another advantage of the waterstart is that you arrive on the board already powered up, moving and therefore far more stable.

From falling to being back up and sailing, no matter how the rig has landed, eventually should take no longer than five seconds. While this will not be the case straight away, it is a realistic goal nonetheless.

WHEN?

Learn to waterstart as soon as possible. Waterstarting demands suppleness and moments of explosive energy. Crucially, it introduces you early on to the fact that windsurfing is not just a jolly pastime but a skill-based, athletic endeavour.

Providing you are a reasonably fit, enthusiastic candidate and the conditions are right, waterstarting can be introduced within two or three months of learning. Why so soon? The barrier to making progress in strong winds is purely mental. Many novices are reluctant to commit themselves to the harness and drive the board because they can't bear the prospect of making a mistake, dropping the rig and then having to heave it back up again. However, knowing that any mistake is redeemable through an immediate and tireless waterstart allows you to embrace the essential concept of success via unbridled experimentation.

Furthermore, the need to be able to climb on to the board, balance at rest, and pull up the rig, keeps people on boards that are often too big for the conditions and the moves they are working on. The sooner you learn to waterstart, the sooner you can experiment with smaller, faster and more manoeuvrable boards.

THE APPROACH

I learned to waterstart by mistake. On a windy day I disappeared out to sea, tried to turn, fell in and climbed back on the board to discover that I had forgotten to attach an uphaul rope. Waterstarting, an almost mythical move at the time, was the only option. Necessity being the mother of invention, I finally managed it and limped home an hour later.

Waterstarting requires the stamina and tenacity of a triathlete … but only if you approach it in the wrong way, at the wrong place with the wrong equipment.

Conditions

The waterstart is unusual in that, to a certain extent, it gets easier as the wind builds. In strong winds, the sail generates so much power that it will heave you up from just about any position, despite less than perfect technique. Lighter winds demand greater agility and more precision. Experts can waterstart in winds as light as 7–10kt (force 3) but for the beginner, an 11–21kt wind (force 4–5) wind is ideal.

Waves, when learning, are a nuisance. They push the board off line, shelter the wind and grab at the sail as you try to release it from the water. Seek out flat water.

The ideal location is a shallow shelving beach where you can stand up inshore and work out the mechanics at your leisure. Treading water is exhausting and, out of your depth, the power of rational thought soon deserts you. The smart plan is to start in your depth and move into deeper and deeper water as your confidence grows until you finally lose all contact with the seabed.

Equipment

A big, wide, thick board is harder to waterstart than a small one. It sits so high in the water that, like climbing up a tall step, you have further to rise. A small board (under 120ltr) sinks beneath you so you can roll up and over it in a small arc. You should practise the watersart on a board that you are familiar with and can actually sail. If, for example, you are forced to practise in deep water, you need to know that you can climb on, pull the rig up in the conventional manner, and sail back if your attempts are unsuccessful.

The waterstart may be broken into three stages. First, there is rig recovery, the act of freeing the rig from the water. Second, just as with the beachstart, the rig is used to manoeuvre the board into position; and third is the act of rising up on to the board.

RIG RECOVERY

Following a seemingly endless variety of gymnastic dismounts, the rig can end up just about anywhere – upwind or downwind of the board with the mast facing the front or back, floating or totally submerged, and so on. Although there are various strategies and short cuts for different situations, the same overriding principle applies to all – let the wind do the work. You cannot release the rig from the water using brute force alone. The only way is to get the wind to blow under the rig and release it for you.

The photo sequence overleaf illustrates the basics but these are the essential points.

- **Orientation**. Be constantly aware of the wind direction. As you surface after a fall, pause, take in the scenery, check the wind and then make a plan.
- **Swim the rig**. It is by inviting air to blow under the sail that you get the wind to 'unstick' the rig from the water. No matter how it is lying, aim to swim the rig around until the mast is at 90 degrees to the wind. The mast is the longest and most stable edge of the sail, so if you lift it from this position, you expose the greatest area of sail to the wind.
- **Handle the mast**. To give yourself the most leverage, grab the rig from near the top of the mast with one hand and use the other to swim. As you swim it round, gently shake the mast up and down and from side to side to drain off some of the water.
- **Release the rig**. To free the rig, you must not lift it straight up but rather keep it quite close to the water and throw the mast towards the wind, which will force enough air under the sail to get the end of the boom to release. You have to be forceful. If the rig fails to fly first time, launch it again, all the time pumping the mast up and down to squeeze the wind underneath.
- **Power up**. As soon as the rig is clear,

Swim to the rig, grab the mast about 1m (3ft) above the boom and start to swim it towards the wind.

Wind
Direction

As you swim, start to shake the mast up and down to feed air under the sail and allow the water to drain off.

With the mast across the wind, release it by keeping it close to the water and pulling it sharply up over your head and into wind. The sudden rush of air under the sail will force it out of the water.

Rig Recovery Sequence (John Carter)

To stop the rig collapsing back down, immediately power it up by placing your hands on the boom in their normal positions and sheeting in.

grab the boom in the normal places and power the rig up. Until you get sheeted in and powered up, you have to tread water and there is a risk of it dropping back in the water.

Alternative Techniques

Just how easily the rig releases depends on how it ends up in the water. Why the pros appear to waterstart so quickly is that, and this will appear a strange concept, they fall well. As soon as they lose balance, they are already planning how and where to land and what to do with the rig so they can push it straight up. This is the order of preference.

1. Try not let go! Especially if you are falling back to windward, keep hold of the boom and as you hit the water, extend the arms high to keep the rig flying.
2. Don't sink it! If an unnoticed gust pulls you forward off balance, try above all to avoid landing on top of the rig. If your plummeting body sinks it, it takes a lot longer to recover. Roll off to one side so the sail ends up flat to the water.
3. Speed! As the rig lands on the water, it traps air underneath and only needs the lightest of flicks to fly it, if you get to it quickly. If you abandon it to have a curse or a rest, water pours into the luff sleeve, small waves wash over the sail and the grimmer the task becomes.

When it Sinks…

You cannot plan all your falls and sometimes you will sink the rig. However, there is no immediate need to reach for an aqualung. Pause for a second and once again let the wind do the work. As the board drifts, the sail will naturally rise to the surface and float horizontally. You can help it on its way by swimming the board to one side.

If the End of the Boom Catches

This is the most common rig recovery malaise. If the rig is not quite free and the end of the boom catches, the sail suddenly fills and is torn from your hands. This is worse in waves and with big sails with long booms. Most of the time, however, it is no more than a symptom of bad technique where you have pushed the mast up vertically to release it rather than throwing it into wind.

If the boom does catch – hang on! Be brutal with it. Grab the mast with both hands and push it back down. Then, with the sail level on the water, try again.

If the end of the boom catches, grab the mast, heave it back down and flatten the sail to the water. Pushing the mast straight up rather than throwing it into wind causes the problem. (John Carter)

Back of the Board Method
Many veteran windsurfers will swear to you that the easiest way to recover the rig is to pull the boom up on to the back of the board. The buoyancy in the tail supports the rig and, hey presto, it's free. It worked on older boards but now we set the booms higher and locate the mastfoot further back, the boom reaches beyond the tail. Although some people lower their booms and put their mast bases forward just so they can waterstart using this method, it ruins the board's trim and performance.

To be truthful, the back of the board method breeds a little laziness. It doesn't work well in all situations, least of all on small boards in waves, so it's just as well to learn the method I described earlier.

Make Life Easy
Treading water like a manic duck, thrusting the sail up with the energy of a leaping salmon … when you're not doing it right, recovering the rig is about the most exhausting exercise known to man. If, having moved from the shallow training ground, you want to try the real thing with your feet off the bottom, a buoyancy vest can save countless calories. However, some people, notably strong swimmers, find they make them top heavy and unstable in the water.

Manoeuvring into Position
With the rig free, the aim now is to end up with the board lying across the wind or just upwind of a beam reach You should be about 1m (3ft) upwind of the board with your back foot resting on the tail between the front and back footstraps.

The manoeuvring technique is the same as for the beachstart: pushing down on the boom bears the nose away from the wind; pulling up on the boom brings the nose closer to the wind.

However, this is a little more complicated in that the board pivots around the fin so the back of the board effectively stays still. So if, for example, the board is lying head to wind and you want to bear it

When the mast is pointing directly into wind, the best tactic is to grab the tip with one hand and the end of the batten with the other. Then, with the strength of a shot-putter, thrust them skywards. By pushing the batten up, you get the wind to feed under the sail.

Wind
Direction

As the sail begins to release, work your way down the mast and sheet in as soon as possible. (John Carter)

away, you have to apply downwards pressure on the boom and then actually swim towards the mastfoot to follow the nose as it moves away.

You can only use this method of steering if you maintain some distance between yourself and the upwind side of the board. The challenge lies in holding your position. Without your feet anchored, you have to keep pumping the legs to stay upwind; otherwise you will just drift in towards the

tail, the board will then spin into wind and the rig will collapse.

The other reason for staying upwind of the board is to give yourself room to lift your back leg on. It requires a little effort to do this from such a low position. As you do so the shoulders tend to drop back and the natural reaction is to hold yourself up by pulling on the boom. Unfortunately, this just pulls the nose into wind and causes the rig to back-wind and drop.

To keep the board on line as you lift the leg, hold the rig high to keep power in the sail and lift the torso up. At the same time, stop the board heading up by swinging the hips and upper body forwards and applying pressure down through the boom and into the mastfoot.

Getting Up
You rise up by getting the rig to produce more power whilst at the same time

To bear the board away and get into the start position, push down on the boom …

Wind Direction

… and swim towards the mastfoot. This is the perfect start position. The board is lying across the wind and you are about 1m (3ft) from the upwind edge, level with the footstraps.

Manoeuvring and Getting Up Sequence
(John Carter)

Lift the back foot on. Place it so the heel is resting on the upwind edge just behind the front footstraps. The act of lifting the leg can make the board head up, so compensate by swinging forward and pushing down on the boom.

Wind
Direction

To rise up, extend the arms up and towards the nose and try to get the rig as upright as possible. With the front arm still extended, the back arm bends to power up the sail. Project the head and upper body forward towards the mastfoot and roll up over a bent back leg.

When the rig is upright, you can pull yourself up under the boom. Be ready to open the sail and ease the power as you rise.

making yourself as small, light and easy to lift as possible. The extra power is generated by extending the arms and throwing the rig as high as possible to expose more sail area to the wind.

You make yourself easy to lift by bending the knees and staying compact. Remember forward rolls from those school PE lessons? To stand up without using your hands, you had to throw your arms and shoulders forward and bend the knees right up to the chest in order to get your weight over your feet before standing up.

However, standing up is not the sole aim. In order to keep the board level as you come up, you have to step forward on the board. The trick is to get the rig as high as possible and then pull yourself up under the boom. So long as the mast is upright, you can pull down on the boom without bringing the whole lot down over your head.

TIMING

Effortless waterstarting comes from exploiting all your lift sources – the wind,

the rig and you – and bringing them together into one explosive moment. Three things happen all at once.

1. Having spotted a gust, pull the tail towards your bottom with your back foot to bear the board away slightly off the wind and increase the power in the sail.
2. Like a spring uncoiling, roll your shoulders forward, extend the front arm and throw the rig up and forwards with the aim of trying to put your nose on the mastfoot.
3. Kick your front leg, the one not yet on the board, to gain that extra bit of lift as you take it out of the water and place it forwards on the board in front of the front footstraps.

Although energy is required, if you 'explode' too fiercely on to the board you can all too easily pile straight over the front. The aim is to rise up sailing and in control. The rig generates a surge of power as it comes vertical, so keep your weight low and be ready to open the sail.

TROUBLESHOOTING

I have devoted a disproportionate amount of words to the waterstart because it is so important not just to be able to do, but to be able to do well. At the upper levels, those making the quickest progress waterstart in seconds with the minimum fuss. As a result they lose little energy and, above all, stay upwind. The longer you spend recovering the rig or getting going, the further you drift downwind.

Problems with waterstarting are usually down to one or another of the following.

Bad Posture

As with all windsurfing moves, going back to basics can usually rectify problems and there is nothing more basic than your stance. Although you are in the water, hold the boom and address the rig just as if you were sailing normally. The most common problem is having the hands too wide apart. The closer together they are, the higher you can stretch the rig. By the same token, if you hold the boom lightly in the fingertips without strangling it, you can stretch the rig even higher.

Wind Unaware

There is no point in trying to explode from the water if the wind has momentarily dropped. Study the water surface upwind of you and time your effort with a gust.

Bad Power Control

Slick waterstarting is not just about creating the power to lift you on, but also about controlling it. Much of that control comes from being aware of the board's angle to the wind. For example, if you bear away too much, especially in a strong wind, the sail will power up and the board will take-off whether you are on it or not. The stronger the wind, the more upwind the board must point during the whole waterstart sequence.

UPHAULING – THE USEFUL ALTERNATIVE

Yes, the waterstart is the gateway to wind-surfing freedom and will change your life

… however, there are occasions when, even on a small board, uphauling is a better option. If you watch a Formula or Olympic race where the competitors are using big rigs (all over 7.5sq m) they will waterstart if they fall hanging on to the rig. However, if they let it go, they will invariably climb on and pull it up rather than try to recover it from the water. Here are other situations where uphauling is favourite.

- If the rig has sunk or is lying awkwardly on the downwind side, a clever tactic is to snap it out of the water in the knowledge that if you fall in backwards with it, you can keep flying it and waterstart back up.
- If it's cold! In winter I uphaul whenever possible. Often in those chilly months, the air temperature is quite bearable but being fully immersed in near-freezing water is not. The less time you spend in it, the longer you can sail.

- When the wind drops. If, after you have flown the rig, you haven't managed to get up after thirty seconds of trying, get on and pull it up.

Although you learned to waterstart to abolish the need for tiresome uphauling, you will find that as your general wind awareness, sailing and power control improves, so will your uphauling, even in a stronger wind and a choppy sea. It is all about technique. For more stability, take up a wider stance with the feet either side of the mastfoot and let the wind do the work. Pull the rig around in the water so the mast is across the wind. As you raise it, the wind will blow under the sail and do much of the lifting for you … but you need to be quick. The crucial tip is not to dally but to 'snap' the rig out of the water before the end of the boom catches and the wind drives it back down.

To illustrate what is possible, the board buckling under the weight of the 87kg (192lb) author has only 100ltr of volume. Adopt a wider stance than usual for stability and take hold of the top of the uphaul rope.

Wind Direction

Let the board drift into wind, then in one motion snap' the rig out of the water, reach for the boom with the back hand and power up the sail, even if the front hand is still on the uphaul. The faster you sheet in the sooner you will have a counterbalance. (Dave White)

CHAPTER 7

SAILING A SMALLER BOARD

Twenty years ago, most short boards never got to see the water. Affluent members of a certain (then) prosperous middle-European country bought them because they looked good on top of the car and afforded their owners instant status at the local lake. Their bluff was hardly ever called, as there was rarely enough wind at these land-locked spots to sail them anyway.

Thankfully, times have changed and it is no longer considered hip to be seen wallowing up to your knees on a board that is too small for the conditions. The cool ones are out there on whatever size of board and rig it takes to get them planing.

While words cannot describe the nerve-jangling thrill of that first planing run on a small board, if you go too small and abandon your big equipment, you risk spending many leisure hours staring at the ocean or being a burden to the rescue services.

THE GLORY OF SMALL

Making the step to a smaller board is like taking the stabilizers off a bicycle – very wobbly to start with, but just as easy to balance once you get a bit of speed up. It

A posse of small boards (100–130ltr), all planing freely in this 17–21kt (force 5) breeze. Initially, your size, skill and training ground will determine how small your board should be. (John Carter)

is more responsive, corners a lot better, and it is only when you slow right down that you wobble. Likewise, a small board is less stable when stationary. However, as it starts to plane and the hull lifts, it turns into a more solid platform, and the faster you go (within reason), the more stable it becomes.

A smaller board is essential if you want to master winds of force 5 (17–21kt) and above. A board of more than 130ltr is very tricky to control in such conditions. It is too buoyant, it hits waves at speed and literally corks out of the water. Worse still, thanks to the larger surface area, a strong wind can literally flip a big board out of the water.

By dropping down a board size, you gain more manoeuvrability and control. With a reduced surface area, the board pushes through the water rather than bouncing off every little lump and it takes minimum pressure to rock it from edge to edge to initiate a turn.

As speed comes primarily from hanging on to a big sail, a smaller board is not necessarily faster, although it certainly feels that way. You are able to make small but spontaneous changes of direction to follow the smoothest line, which allows you to make faster and more controlled progress in wilder conditions.

REALITY CHECK

There is no fundamental difference between sailing the biggest and the smallest boards. If you were to watch a close-up of an experienced windsurfer starting, accelerating and then sailing, his technique would not reveal the size of board he was on. The way you address the rig, control the power, trim and drive the board is the same.

Although there is no need to learn anything new, sailing a smaller board forces you to become a better windsurfer as it immediately exposes bad and unsubtle technique. However, before we look at the technicalities, let me offer two essential pieces of advice.

Make a Sensible Drop

How small is small? How much should you drop down? So much depends on how well you already sail the bigger board; on your size, fitness and determination; on whether you can waterstart and the area of water where you are most likely to practise.

This simple equation will help you. A litre of volume supports a kilogram of weight. To be stable in light winds, the board needs at least 100ltr of reserve volume. Therefore, if you weigh 80kg (176lb), you need a board with around 180ltr of volume.

For an easy rite of passage, your first small board needs about 40ltr of reserve volume. So our 80kg windsurfer would be looking at a board of around 120ltr, which is still buoyant enough to stand on and pull the rig without calling on any advanced skills but has the following small-board design features:

You step on a small board (100ltr in this case) in the knowledge that if you do put a foot in the wrong place, you're going down! (Dave White)

Standing on the upwind side of the board, hold the windward front footstrap with the front hand, the top of the boom with the other and let the wind get under both. This is good for walking into and across the wind.

Wind
Direction

Wind
Direction

Stand between the board and rig, holding the top of the boom with one hand and a front footstrap with the other. This works walking across the wind but is especially effective downwind.

Three Carrying Techniques
(John Carter and Dave White)

Holding the windward front footstrap with the back hand and the mast with the other, incline the rig right down to windward over your head and lift.

Wind
Direction

This is the trickiest but most effective method, especially when launching in surf as you can hold everything high above the waves. It works across and into wind but is not possible when facing downwind.

- No daggerboard or central fin – just a relatively small rear fin.
- No training footstraps.
- Very unstable at rest and, at first, impossibly sensitive to weight transfer.

Training Grounds

As you prepare for your maiden voyage on a small board, look downwind because that is where you are going to end up. There is no reason to be downhearted about this or regard it as a failing, just accept that it will happen. Initially, everything is stacked against you sailing upwind. It will take you longer to uphaul or waterstart and during this time you will drift downwind. The small fin offers very little resistance at slow speeds and the sail produces relatively little forward force upwind, so you will find yourself having to bear away just to stay on the plane.

The choice of training ground plays an important part. At the ideal spot, the wind will be constant, the water smooth and shallow. The depth of the water is very important at this stage because you will probably only be able to summon up the confidence to attack in the knowledge that you can stand in your depth if anything goes wrong. If you are worried about where you may end up, you tighten up and the learning process ceases.

GENERAL TRIM AND BALANCE

Sailing a short board demands a different sort of balance. Obviously, it is much more sensitive to weight shift. Soon, however, you will regard this as an advantage as it takes only a dab of the toe or heel to level it out in choppy conditions. By contrast, a big board will absorb errant footsteps but, if it does start to tip, you have to make a mighty lunge in the other direction to rectify the situation.

Apart from the general need to develop more sensitive feet, there are three main differences between sailing a small and a big board.

First, there are very few choices about where you can put your feet on a short board. If you are off the plane, you must have the front foot alongside or in front of the mast with the back foot behind it across the centreline. If you sheet out with both feet behind the mast, the tail will sink. The most comfortable and most secure position on a small board is planing with both feet in the straps.

Second is anticipation – this has always been important but now it is vital. Things happen so much faster on a small board that if you fail to anticipate the changes in wind and sail pressure, it is usually too late. The classic case is that of getting trapped in the straps. If you run into an extended lull on a big board, you can get away with staying in the straps. On a smaller board, unless you move smartly forward, you will sink. So many falls are avoidable if you keep one eye on the wind, the other on the water ahead.

Last, the sinking feeling. Rejoice in the fact that a small board sinks a little at rest.

All the wave action is on the surface – a big board sits right on the surface and so is buffeted by every undulation but a small board sits in the calmer water beneath. Try to balance without moving your feet, stand up with your hips forward and the centre of gravity over your feet – avoid over-reaction and all will be well.

EARLY PLANING

Small boards are slower to get going because they sit deeper in the water and therefore need more power to lift them up on to their planing surface. While the amateur will need a wind speed of 17–21kt (force 5) and a 6.5sq m sail to grind his 120ltr board into action, a professional of the same weight will probably manage to pop his 85ltr wave board with a 5.7sq m sail on to the plane in just 11–16kt (force 4) of wind. Yes, it's all about technique (and a little about fitness too).

As you improve, you will be able to make the same board and rig combination plane in less and less wind. How early you can plane is a true barometer of windsurfing skill – and how much weight you are losing!

The aim is to present the board at an angle to the water where it causes the least resistance and the rig at an angle to the wind where it produces the most power. You then have to distribute the force of the sail into exactly the right parts of the board to drive it forward. At the same time, you must adjust your weight and move your feet in such a way that they never disrupt the overall trim or prevent the board from rising up.

This is the moment to grasp what actually drives a board along and what forces come into play as you accelerate.

A BALANCING ACT

The power of the rig is transferred into the board through your feet and the mastfoot. How you distribute these forces determines whether the board rides level or whether it drags its nose or tail. Effectively, it is a see-saw with the fulcrum between the front straps and the mastfoot. These are the ways to share the power.

- **With your body.** If you swing your hips and upper body towards the nose and hang off the boom, you will direct the load away from your feet and into the mastfoot.
- **Through the board angle to the wind.** If you bear away, the power in the sail and therefore the load directed into the mastfoot increases (nose down). As you head up towards the wind, the rig produces less power, less force goes through the mastfoot, the shift of balance moves to the feet and the tail sinks.
- **The sheeting angle.** Sheeting in and out has the same effect as controlling the

In this solid 22–27kt (force 6) wind, there is plenty of power to push the 100ltr board on to the plane: the issue is controlling it. Rather than sheet out, the best strategy is to stay close to the wind. Hook in with the feet forward of the straps.

Getting into Straps on a Small Board (John Carter)

Wind Direction

By staying close to the wind you reduce the forward pull in the rig, so as you lift the front foot into the strap, lean forward in the harness to direct your weight into the mastfoot and hold the nose down.

Before the board fully releases on to the plane, quickly slip the back foot into its strap and then gradually bear away to get up to full speed.

Wind Direction

Windsurfers flying over the handlebars due to a sudden change in their apparent wind direction is a magnificent sight.

power through the board angle to the wind, as described above. Sheeting in increases the power into the mastfoot, sheeting out cuts it off.

From a standing start through to stepping back into the straps and rising on to the plane, your simple aim is to trim the board level and to direct a constant flow of power into the board. A small board does not have the volume to absorb unplanned jolts. Any bullish movements with either the rig or feet will be met with a sudden change of trim, much spray and violent braking.

The fundamentals are the same as for getting a big board to plane but certain elements are especially important.

- **Commit to the harness**. Hook in early on a close reach. Once the shoulders and hips drop back to engage the line, that is where they stay. Feel that constant flow of power through the line in the knowledge that if you drop inboard and the line goes slack, the board will lurch to a stop.

- **Rig forward/mast upright**. When the rig is forward and upright it drives the nose down and keeps the board level as it accelerates. If you drag it back, it will sink the tail. Because the small board is initially creating more drag as it rises up, there is more force in the rig. Resist the temptation to drag it back and 'dig in'. Hold it forward and away from you on extended arms in the knowledge that the power will soften as the board accelerates. Like the racehorse that is ready to bolt, loosen the reins and give it its head!

- **Bear away**. The general rule is that because small boards need more power to make them plane, you should bear further off the wind as you get going (the sail produces more power on a broad reach). However, if it is windy, just the opposite is true. Many problems stem from people trying to get into the straps when the board is already going too fast. Sometimes the best strategy is to stay close to the wind as you step back and only bear away when your feet are secure in the straps.

- **On your toes**. Imitate the ballet dancer. Imagine you weigh a mere 45kg (100lb). Pretend the board is made of the finest bone china. In other words, stay on your toes as the board is accelerating and make yourself as light as you can. As you step back into the straps, slide the feet into place and make every weight shift as subtle as possible.

- **Weight on the rig**. To allow the board to rise on to its tail, you have to get the weight off your feet. As you step back, compensate by dropping all your weight into the harness and hanging off the boom.

- **Trim trim trim**. The back foot has a particularly crucial role in keeping the board level in the sideways plane. Place it just behind the front straps, straddling the centreline. As you put the front foot in its strap (which is on the windward side), compensate and hold the board level by pressing on the toes of the back foot.

WHAT REALLY HAPPENS...

The wondrous, shocking, thrilling aspect about this first foray on a small board is how sudden the acceleration is. One second you are doing barely 3kph (2mph), the next, with no apparent warning, the booster rockets ignite and you find yourself overtaking jet skis. Unless you are hooked in, in the straps and generally secure in your stance, it will feel like being on a rollercoaster with the safety bar still up.

Most problems stem from wayward feet. People delay too long and try to move the feet into the footstraps when already fully planing. With so little of the board in contact with the water, any major foot movement at this stage causes dynamic upset. You have to move the feet subtly – but also swiftly and positively. On no account look down. If you do, the shoulders drop forward, tension comes off the harness line, the sail will de-power and stop. Look ahead and feel for the footstraps.

PUMPING

Originally banned in racing as an unfair way to propel the board, pumping is actually an act of great skill and your most potent early planing weapon. By moving the sail in and out, you can create an artificial gust and pulse of power strong enough to make the board release on to the plane. Pumping takes various forms.

Pumping the Rig in the Harness

The sail creates power and lift through air passing over its foil. Air is actually quite sticky stuff. As you sheet in to get going, it can get trapped in the sail and swirl round in vortexes, killing the power. Hooked in, just pump the sail in and out with the back hand. The action gets the leech to twist open, encourages the trapped air to escape and the normal laminar flow to re-establish itself.

Pumping the Board

This is energetic stuff. You can stay hooked in but you will get more leverage if you unhook. Start just off the wind and hold the rig forward on straight arms.

Without moving the rig too much, tug the boom aggressively with both arms, thrust the hips forward and direct that pulse of power through the feet and into the board, pointing the toes to shoot it forward. The board will sink a little under the pressure then cork back up to the surface. You should repeat the action three, four, five or however many times is necessary to bounce it up on to its planing surface.

Warning!

Pumping can also be a reliable way to ensure you never plane. Done well, it is almost balletic in its rhythm and efficiency. Done badly, you will look and sound like a dying swan as your sail flaps impotently atop a sinking board.

IN A STRAIGHT LINE

Although the fundamentals of stance and trim are the same for any board, you do have to adapt certain aspects of your game to get the most out of small boards.

Smaller Fin

Boards of more than about 150ltr will carry huge fins of 45cm and above. Their function is to resist the considerable sideways force of a big sail and assist early planing in medium winds. As soon as you start to move, you can feel the fin connect and if you drive against it, even at relatively slow speeds, you get a positive reaction. The fin turns your drive into lift and away you go.

On a smaller board, the role of the fin is primarily to offer you control at high speed and to help the board hold in the water through fast turns. A 100ltr board will probably be fitted with a fin of only about 30cm. On a small wave board it may be as small as 19cm. Both need a considerable water flow over them before they will start to lift. If you hoof against a small fin at slow speeds, it will just slew sideways and 'spin out'.

Spin Out

You may be sailing quite normally when suddenly your fin loses its grip on the water, the tail breaks away and you slide sideways, completely out of control.

Pushing too hard, at too slow a speed against a small fin often causes spin out. It

can also be caused by air getting trapped under the board and attaching itself to the fin – this is known as 'ventilation' and is usually the result of bad trim. Sloppy power control and heavy feet make the board bounce. A good sailor will plaster the board to the water with constant foot and mastfoot pressure to stop the air channelling underneath.

The main culprit, however, is the back foot. You can push hard against the fin at high speeds so long as the pressure is constant, but shock loads will cause a problem. The easiest way to spin out is to land too heavily on the back foot when you come down from a jump.

Spin Out Correction

If you find that you are skidding sideways, the first priority is to push on the heels to stop the downwind edge from catching and launching you into a 'high-side' catapult fall (motorcyclists will empathize). Unhook and hang off the boom, throwing all your weight outboard and forward into the mastfoot. As the board slows down, use the back foot to pull the tail upwind. As the board straightens up, the fin will find its grip.

THE APPARENT WIND

The 'apparent' wind is the combination of the 'true' wind as produced by nature, and the headwind produced by you moving through the air. The classic illustration is that of the ocean liner. At rest, the smoke from its funnels blows in the direction of the true wind, which, in this example, is at right angles to the ship. As the ship moves forward, its headwind and the true wind combine, and the smoke starts to flow diagonally backwards.

The apparent wind direction changes every time your speed and/or the wind speed changes. As you trim your sail to the apparent wind so you must be aware of this changing direction and strength. Here are a few examples of how apparent wind affects your approach on big and small boards.

• **Sail angle**. As you accelerate, the apparent wind direction moves forward so you have to sheet in more to keep the sail powered. Your experience in light winds tells you to hold the boom away from you on a broad reach to present the sail to the wind. But if you are planing fast, the apparent wind direction will flow forward. If you are sailing fast relative to the wind speed, there may be times when you will have the sail sheeted right in over the centreline even though you are travelling downwind.

- **Sail through the lulls**. Imagine that you are planing along and you see a group of boards ahead lying stationary in a lull. Amazingly, you keep planing straight past them. The explanation is that although the true wind had dropped, the apparent wind was still flowing over the sail, giving enough lift to keep you going. To maintain that flow, you have to hold the rig still as you sail into a lull.
- **Power surges and catapults**. Small boards decelerate as suddenly as they accelerate and you have to be aware of the effect this has on your apparent wind. If, for example, you slam into a small wave and slow right down, the apparent wind direction will suddenly swing back creating a forward pull in the sail strong enough to heave you out of the straps. If you do slow down, be ready to ease out the back hand to dump the power.

SAILING UPWIND

If early planing is one barometer of windsurfing skill, the ability to sail a short board upwind in all conditions is another. As these boards, even the ones with the smallest fins, have the potential to sail very close to the wind at huge speed, you must be more tuned into the conditions and especially sensitive to board and rig trim.

Big boards make us lazy. To sail upwind on or off the plane, all you have to do is point and go while the daggerboard and/or big fin do the rest of the work. On a smaller board, the fin only provides lift and resistance when the board is fully planing. Therein lies the secret: speed is your biggest upwind weapon!

You have to bear away to get right up to speed before gradually heading up, but this is something people are reluctant to do for fear of losing even more ground.

Upwind Stance

As you head upwind from a beam reach, the sail produces less and less forward drive and more and more sideways drag. You have to compensate for the drop in force going through the mastfoot by swinging the hips forward and powering down through the rig. The feeling is one of literally shoving the board forward. Angle the rig back and then drive the whole body forward so your head is almost level with the mastfoot. There is a two-point contact – the back foot is driving against the fin while your weight is driving into the mastfoot. The front foot is barely weighted.

Reading the Conditions

Upwind, an experienced windsurfer will power ahead of a lesser sailor because he reads and reacts to the conditions – wind is the cherished weapon. If he sees a gust ahead, he will gather a little speed and then drive harder off the back foot and point higher. If he feels the pressure in the sail drop and the fin start to skip sideways, he will ease off the pressure on the back foot and bear away to get more speed again. If he is travelling with the waves or swell, he will always try to manoeuvre on to the front of one and then head up along it, using its power to carry him higher.

Off the plane, many waste ground by bumbling off downwind. Always be aware of your sailing course. If you do drop off the plane, you can still make ground, even on a short board. Just stand up near the mastfoot, rock back on your heels and push in the upwind edge to create the same kind of resistance as a daggerboard, and steer upwind. As soon as you see or feel a gust, bear away again to get planing. Your upwind path is invariably a series of loops and curves to exploit the gusts, the lulls and the changes in wind direction – it's rarely a straight line.

SAILING DOWNWIND

Although sailing downwind on a small board is the best ride at the fair, it is the one that few people choose to go on. This is mainly because they lack confidence in their ability to get back upwind, but also because the speed at which they would find themselves moving within just a few seconds is not an experience for the faint-hearted.

The world speed sailing record of 46.3kt was set in force 10 storm conditions (48–55kt), sailing at 140 degrees to the wind. Amateur speedsters crack up and down across the wind with verve and gusto, probably reaching 20kt in a 17–21kt (force 5) wind. That feels fast. But if they were to bear away just 30 degrees, so long as they were carrying a big enough sail, they would be clocking nearer 30kt. When the wind is from your rear quarter, the sail works most efficiently. Its full area is given to the wind and it produces very little sideways drag.

As for your technique and posture, the fundamentals are the same. Keep the hips and upper body parallel with the boom; hold the rig forward and away from you on extended arms and trim the board flat and level. The overall feeling, however, is quite different.

With the wind from behind, the rig pulls you forward towards the nose. You resist by leaning back towards the tail, not to windward. Your centre of gravity is neaerer to the centreline. The fear factor comes from the fact that you are not only moving faster but, should you get hit by an unforeseen gust, you are likely to get pulled forward on top of the rig.

Downwind, the load moves more to the front foot. As you bear away and the rig pulls you inboard and forward, straighten the front leg and brace yourself against it. Actively drive the board through the chop (small, irregular waves moving out from the source of the wind) and stop the nose lifting.

Try not to get defensive. Sheeting out and dropping back, the two most instinctive means of self-preservation, are the ones most likely to land you in trouble. If you ease off the power suddenly at speed, you cut off the power to the mastfoot, the nose will be thrust into the air by the first piece of chop and you will either spin out or bounce into a heap. The way to slow

As you change course, the sail pulls from a different direction and you have to alter your stance accordingly. Here, sailing across the wind, everything is fairly symmetrical. Both legs are just slightly flexed with more or less equal pressure on both feet.

Sailing upwind, the forward pressure in the sail drops, so to keep the board tracking level, angle the rig back and lean the hips and torso forward until your head is level with the mastfoot. The feeling is that of shoving the board upwind with the rig. The load moves to the back foot. If you are powered up, drive off it to maximize the lift from the fin.

Wind Direction

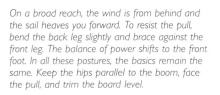

On a broad reach, the wind is from behind and the sail heaves you forward. To resist the pull, bend the back leg slightly and brace against the front leg. The balance of power shifts to the front foot. In all these postures, the basics remain the same. Keep the hips parallel to the boom, face the pull, and trim the board level.

A Stance for all Wind Directions (John Carter)

down is to lean on the heels and head into wind, at the same time gradually easing out the back hand. After a couple of falls, the instinctive reaction is to heave the rig back, drop down and roll up into a ball like a startled hedgehog. But if you direct too much power through the back foot, the board will drag on its tail, skip and slow down. Ironically, the more you slow down, the harder the sail pulls.

Sailing fast off the wind is scary because it's a leap into the known. The only sensible approach is to extend that comfort zone by nibbling at the task ahead. Initially, just bear away a few degrees and stay sheeted in for about five seconds. Then go a bit broader for a little longer until finally you are doing mile-long stretches with both hands off the boom. The reality is that sailing fast off the wind on a lumpy ocean takes considerable skill and courage – on flat water the task is disproportionately easier.

When strong winds send you up to warp speed, the instinctive reaction is to throw out the anchor. However, if you hook out and sheet out, you cut off the power to the nose and the board rears up like a startled stallion.

Instead, think about lowering your stance (the head is now below the boom), staying committed to the harness and driving the board on to the water. (John Carter)

CHAPTER 8

GYBING

There is a multitude of gybes with whacky prefixes such as 'monkey', 'back-wind', 'pirouette' and 'Essex duck'. However, there are actually just two fundamental techniques for turning a board downwind. One is for mostly non-planing conditions where you steer the board round with the rig. The other is where you bank the board over with foot pressure and carve it round using its own momentum. For this, the board must be planing.

These techniques are not specific to board size and the proficient windsurfer will have mastered both. As you improve, you will naturally aspire to the planing carve gybe but you still need to be able to manoeuvre safely and quickly if the wind drops.

The problem with all the basic moves described in Chapter 2 is that they take too long. As you take your tacks and gybes on to rougher water and smaller boards, stability becomes a major issue. The longer you delay in mid-transition without power in the sail, the more vulnerable you are. With the sail powered, you have a counterbalance; so the sooner you get round

The gybe starts across the wind. Step back towards the tail, slide the back hand down the boom and initiate the gybe by tilting the rig to windward (the outside of the turn).

Wind Direction

As the board turns through the wind, push the back hand away to open the sail. As the sail pivots round, follow it with your body. The front foot pivots round first …

Non-Planing Gybe Sequence *(John Carter)*

... then the back foot turns and steps forward right up to the mastfoot. You are now holding the sail 'clew first'.

Wind Direction

To flip the rig round, slide the front hand to the front of the boom, release the back hand and cross it over to the front of the new side of the boom.

Move the front hand to the middle of the boom and pull on the power.

and sheet in again on the new tack, the better your chances of success. It is also important to keep the board moving. The faster it travels through the turn, the more stable it is. Be sure to move the feet to their new positions deftly yet positively so they spend the minimum amount of time off the centreline.

THE FLARE GYBE

Inspired by the sight of the nose 'flaring' skywards like a rearing horse, the flare gybe has become the generic term for a non-planing gybe that is usually performed on a big board in light or moderate winds. You would spring right to the tail in an attempt to get the board vertical, spin it round and then rush forward again to kill the rotation.

The rig provides the turning force. Think for a moment of canoeing. If you want to turn left, you paddle on the right side of the boat. The further you stretch the blade away from the side of the boat and the harder you pull, the greater the turning force and the faster you spin. The

same principle applies to the flare gybe. The rig is your paddle – to turn left, lean the rig to the right. Off the plane, the full length of the board sits in the water and resists the turn. To free it up, you move back and get the nose to lift out. As if on a turntable, the board can then spin round on the tail alone.

Familiarize yourself with a couple of new turning reference terms – 'inside' and 'outside'. Imagine the turn as a circle. 'Inside' means towards the centre of the turning circle. 'Outside' is away from the turning circle. The inside edge (the one engaged in a carving turn) is the one nearest the centre of the circle. The outside edge is the one furthest away.

The exact technique changes depending on whether the daggerboard (if fitted) is up or down. If the daggerboard is up, you keep the board level as you lean on the back foot to sink the tail and create a pivot. If the daggerboard is down, you press in the outside edge as you step back – press right to turn left. This is known as 'opposite rail steering' and only works if you are far back on the board and have

sunk the tail enough to raise the daggerboard partially out of the water.

Flare gybing with the daggerboard down is effective up to about a wind speed of 7–10kt (force 3). Thereafter it generates so much lift that it makes the board turn too fast and tips it over. This also applies to a small board, so I would advise practising without the daggerboard.

There are four essential parts to this gybe – the way you move your body to withstand the various forces, the rig action, sailing clew first and the rig flip.

Body Management

The non-planing gybe throws up two apparently conflicting demands on your body. The lower body, from the hips downwards, leans into the turn to

> **TOP TIP**
>
> *The ability to bend and rotate at the hips is key to advanced windsurfing as it allows the knees and ankles to trim and drive the board whilst the upper body controls the rig during all stages of a manoeuvre.*

The key to gybing in all wind conditions is encapsulated here – freedom and suppleness allow the upper and lower body to work independently to keep balance and control the rig. The head, meanwhile, looks to the new direction. (John Carter)

withstand the centrifugal force, whilst the upper body turns to the outside to face the pull in the rig. This demands extreme angulation at the hips so the side of the body forms a 'C' shape.

Rig Action

For the rig to produce a turning force, it has to be consistently powered up. To keep the rig powered all the way round, you have to constantly alter its angle as the board is turning – this is true of all gybes.

Be aware of the wind direction and remember always to present the sail area to the wind. As you bear away and lean to the outside of the turn, sheet the back hand in. Then, as you turn downwind, open the back hand out and keep opening it as you turn through the wind so you end up in the clew first position.

Clew First

The clew is the rear bottom corner of the sail. Sailing 'clew first' means that the sail is switched or the wrong way round, an integral part of countless tricks and turns. Strangely, the sail still produces a forward driving force but feels far less stable and efficient. All the basic controls are reversed – what was the back hand becomes the front hand, but it still controls the sheeting angle and therefore the power. The difference this time is that to power up the rig, you push it away and to de-power you pull it towards you.

Sailing clew first is a challenge that increases exponentially as the wind increases. A wind of 11–16kt (force 4) will make the rig start to tug and gyrate like a pig in a sack. The trick lies in staying off the wind. As you turn upwind, the wind hits the leech (normally the back edge of the sail) first. The leech is unsupported by the mast and readily gets pulled out of shape. The task immediately becomes easier if you keep the mast upright and between you and the front of the board. Slide your back hand (your normal back hand) towards the clew for greater leverage and control.

It is from the clew first position that you perform the rig flip.

Rig Flip

The 'rig flip' or 'rig change' is the act of swinging the rig round from one side to the other. This relatively simple task is the breeding ground for dreadful habits. There are a few options as to exactly where and when you move each hand. I have demonstrated the popular 'boom-to-boom'

This 'boom-to-boom' rig change starts from the clew-first position. Hold the rig forward so the mast is vertical and remains between you and the front of the board.

The front hand is the hinge, so slide it to the front of the boom. The rig can then pivot in front of you.

Release the back hand, cross it over the front hand ...

Wind
Direction

... grab the front of the new side of the boom. The wind and the force of the rotation will combine to blow the rig downwind, so make an effort to hold it upright.

As you sheet in, throw the rig forward on extended arms so the power drives the board level.

Rig Change Sequence *(Dave White)*

change. However, the principles are the same whatever style you use.

The aim is to get your hands into their sailing positions on the new side of the boom with the fewest number of movements. The longer it takes to power up the sail on the new side, the more you slow down and the greater your chances of a fall.

Hold the mast upright as the rig pivots round. If you let it drop to leeward (downwind) it will always pull you off balance on to your toes. If the rig is to drive the board forward after the flip, it must be upright and forward. If it is inclined backwards or downwind, it will just drive you into wind. During the whole process, keep your upper body still and manoeuvre the rig around you. The moment you bend at the waist or lunge to reach the new side of the boom, the game is over. Grip the boom lightly and let your hands be mobile on the boom – when you cling on for dear life, the rig will end up in the wrong place.

THE CARVE GYBE

It was at the Weymouth speed trials of 1981. In this era, windsurfers were still something of a joke entry, lagging some 15kt behind the fastest yachts. But that year, a colourful German by the name of Jurgen Honschied arrived unannounced with a couple of modified surfboards. Although shorter boards were beginning to hit the scene, there had been nothing as small as these.

A gale was blowing. He plugged a tiny rig into the smaller of the two boards; launched, did a waterstart (a novelty in itself), shot off down the 500m (550yd) course and clocked a time of 24kt. Impressive though this speed was, it was not what he was remembered for that day.

At the end of the course, we expected him to stop and hitch a ride back to the start – but no. Instead, he just banked his board over and shot round through 180 degrees, throwing up a mountainous plume of spray like a slalom water-skier. Somehow he moved his feet round, flipped the rig, and in the blink of an eye, he was flying off in the opposite direction. It had no name at the time but we had just seen the first carve gybe. Jaws dropped. In the space of five seconds, Jurgen had taken windsurfing to a different level.

I cannot think of any move in any other sport that captures the imagination and dominates the lives of its participants quite

The carve gybe fixates people to such an extent that you feel it must have been part of some ancient courting ritual. (John Carter)

like the carve gybe. Why? It offers the same adrenaline rush as turning a surfboard on the face of a wave but is more accessible. What is more, the carve gybe is intriguingly frustrating. It seems straightforward until you try it and realize that a number of precise actions need to happen at speed in a very short space of time. Amidst scenes of joy and elation, you complete one; then just when you think you have a handle on it, the wind changes, the water becomes choppier and you find yourself back in the nursery. Consistent perfection seems to remain an eternal and elusive quest. However, on those special occasions when technique, skill, a timely wave and a favourable gust combine harmoniously to produce a cracker, the thrill and satisfaction are immeasurable.

In essence, the carve gybe is simpler than the flare gybe. Planing, you bank the board over on to its inside edge. As it carves through the wind, you flip the sail, turn the feet through 180 degrees and away you go again. That sounds almost flippantly easy. Yet the reason why most people fail is that they over-complicate it. Concentrating too hard on the minutiae brings about paralysis by analysis whereas success in this and many other so-called complicated moves comes from focusing on the basics.

Later, I will try and pick out the classic problem areas and offer a few training tips.

To begin with, try to relate to the photo sequence below and let me pick out the essential point from each of the stages.

Preparation

Here is where the game is won and lost. Make life easy by selecting the best gybing arena – a flat patch of water, in between waves or near to a shore caressed by a constant wind.

Preparation involves checking upwind, downwind and behind for potential crash victims, sliding the back hand down the boom for leverage and placing the back foot just in front of its strap on the inside rail. The goal is to do all that without upsetting either the board or sail trim.

Prepare for the gybe across the wind before bearing away. Check the road is clear, slide the back hand down the boom, unhook and place the back foot on the inside edge.

Wind Direction

Gently pressure the inside edge to bear away and let the increased power in the rig pull you forward and inboard.

Switch-Foot Carve Gybe *(Dave White)*

Now for the carve! Bank the board with foot pressure. Extend the front arm to drop the rig forward and to the inside and bend the back arm to keep it sheeted in.

Wind
Direction

As you turn downwind, increase the pressure on the edge to tighten the turn and sheet out to keep the sail exposed to the wind.

Through the wind, release the back hand to initiate the rig flip and cross it over the front hand to take hold of the new side of the boom.

Still carving with the feet in their original positions, grab the boom and sheet in as it comes within reach. Twist at the hips – knees pointing in, shoulders facing out, body still committed to the turn. To finish, turn the feet through 180 degrees.

You must then delay a couple of seconds to let the board settle before going for it. Many unhook and then carve the board in one motion, sending the board into a bouncing frenzy. Sailing at speed out of the harness is something of an art. Bend the knees to lower your centre of gravity and hang right away from the rig on extended arms like an ape so that much of

TOP TIP

Accept the simple notion that if you don't start the gybe settled, comfortable and with plenty of speed, you certainly aren't going to end it that way. Preparation is everything.

the power from the rig is taken by the back muscles.

Anticipation

On a bicycle, you approach a corner by first leaning over into the turn and then gently turning the handlebars knowing full well that, if you turn the handlebars first, you will be flung off to the outside. The carve gybe involves an equally sudden change in direction, which, if you fail to anticipate it, will leave you falling off the tail, groping for balance.

Let me put it another way. Imagine that you are standing on a rug when somebody grabs one end and gives it a tug. Your feet shoot forward of your body and you col-

lapse painfully on your bottom. You get back on your feet but this time take up a different position. Aware of your 'friend's' evil intentions, you start to lean forwards, dropping your shoulders and hips in front of your feet to the point where you topple forward. When he pulls the rug this time, your feet catch up with your body and you stay in balance.

This is exactly what has to happen in the carve gybe, nearly all of which fall short of perfection because people start and end up too far back on the board. Every aspect of the gybe – the carve, the foot change and the rig change will suffer unless you get your weight forward from the start. The key to anticipation is to bear

Wind Direction

The start is the same as the switch foot gybe. Open the sail out as you carve through the wind.

Step Gybe Sequence *(Dave White)*

This time, change feet before flipping the rig.
Holding the sail clew first, twist the front foot out
of its strap ...

Wind
Direction

... and step the back foot forward of the straps.
Then immediately flip the rig.

Sheet in on the new side with the feet still
forward of the straps.

away a little off the wind and then let the increased power in the rig pull you forward and inboard.

The Carve

This the fun part – pressuring the inside edge, feeling it bite into the water, banking over to show the underside of your board to all upwind of you and taking up the extreme posture needed to counteract the centrifugal forces.

Just as with normal sailing, you get the board to bank over and then carve smoothly by sharing the forces between the feet and the mastfoot. By dropping to the inside of the turn and leaning down on

Hips.
The hips represent the centre of gravity and lead the body into the turn. If the hips hang back, your weight will be back and you will fall off the tail. Look down and you should see the harness hook over the inside rail, level with the inside front strap.

Head.
The body follows the head, so look to the inside of the turning circle, not at the feet.

Shoulders.
Bend slightly at the waist so the shoulders are in front of the hips and feet. Throughout the gybe, the shoulders stay parallel with the boom.

Knees.
The knees must be bent so the legs can extend and retract like pistons to absorb the chop and alter the turning circle. In a committed position the front knee will be over the inside edge and the back knee will almost be touching the foot of the sail.

Ankles.
By bending the ankles you get the rest of the body to drop forward. Check the shins: if they are inclined forward then the ankles are bending; if they are vertical, the ankles are blocked and you will be leaning back.

Feet.
Place the back foot just in front of its straps so the feet are at least shoulder-width apart for stability. The back foot needs to be across the centreline so the toes can pressure the inside edge but not too far over or they will drag in the water. Keep the weight on the balls of the feet, which should remain in contact with the board.

What the various body parts are up to during the carve. (Dave White)

the boom, you control the nose; by pressuring the back foot, you control the tail. The distribution of weight between the front and back foot depends on the width of the board. I will explain how to adjust the technique later.

The key to carving lies quite simply on even pressure. Think of the arc you want to describe. Like the racing driver following the racing line around a bend, the aim is to go in wide and come out tight. The pressure you exert on the edge should be constant and always increasing until you flatten the board off at the end of the turn.

The Role of the Rig

The main difference between this and the non-planing flare gybe is that the rig does not provide the turning force. Like a speedboat, it just produces the power to pull you through the turn.

Take the rig away and the carve gybe would be easy. The rig confuses matters because it pulls and everything you have done in windsurfing up until this point has involved leaning back to resist it. However, in the carve gybe you have to lean towards the direction of the pull. The reason why you are not pulled off balance is that while the rig pulls you forward to start with, as you turn downwind, the headwind cancels out the true wind and the rig goes light; very shortly after that you release it to initiate the rig flip.

The easiest way to explain the rig angle through the gybe is to imagine that you have no UJ and that the mast is bolted directly into the board; so as the board banks over, the rig banks over with it. Although in more advanced gybes you can get pretty active with the rig, thinking of board and rig moving as one unit helps you keep the rig forward and in front of you.

The arms and hands are responsible for holding the rig in position and have very different roles. The front arm is extended in its normal stance and stays extended as the upper body moves forward and inboard to start the carve. The back hand is placed back on the boom about 45cm (18in) behind the rear harness fixing so it

has the leverage to pull in the rig and keep it powered as you bear away. Then as you pass through downwind, just as in the flare gybe, it eases out the boom and finally releases it into the rig change.

The Rig and Foot Change

The basic carve gybe has two forms, the 'step gybe' and 'strap-to-strap gybe', otherwise known as the 'switch foot gybe'. The beginning of each is the same; only the timing of the foot and rig change is different.

In the step gybe you move the feet first, 'stepping' them in front of the straps; then you flip the rig. In the switch foot gybe, you flip the rig first and power it up on the new side with the feet still in their original positions. It is only at this point that you change them and, if you wish, move them straight into the new set of straps.

This image captures the very essence of the carve gybe. The rig has just been released and the board is gliding around on its inside edge under its own momentum. (Dave White)

Although the timings are slightly different, the essential points are the same for both gybes:

- **Keep carving**. It is easy to get distracted during the foot and rig change and stand up and stop carving. Keep the pressure on the rail during the whole transition.
- **Go early**. Although it looks as if the foot and rig change happen at the end of the gybe, you actually start sheeting out into the rig change dead downwind when the gybe is just two seconds old.
- **Tiptoes**. The key to the foot change is to imagine you are treading on eggshells and make the steps and weight transfer as light and subtle as possible.
- **Mast upright**. Whichever gybe you do, just before you flip the rig, slide the front hand to the front of the boom by the mast. The hand then acts like a hinge and the rig swings round in front of you.
- **Hand movement**. Like the flare gybe, the key to the rig change is to make the minimum of hand movements and get powered up on the new side as quickly as possible.

Which Gybe?

To cope with all conditions and board sizes, ultimately you will need to be able to perform both the step and switch-foot gybes. Which one you choose depends on your circumstances and your whim. Here are the pros and cons of each.

Step Gybe

The step gybe is the most versatile technique of the two. Because you hold on to the sail longer and exit in the clew first position, you can rescue gybes where the wind has dropped in mid-arc and use the rig to steer you out. Getting the foot forward earlier helps you to control the nose in choppy conditions and keep the board level in marginal winds. As a result, it is the preferred gybe for boards exceeding 130ltr and sails bigger than 7.5sq m.

The disadvantage is that there is a lot going on all at once. It is quite easy to do one badly and survive, but to get a good exit and keep your planing speed requires precise timing and accurate foot placement.

Switch-Foot Gybe

Because the feet remain still until the end of the gybe, you can concentrate on holding the carving position and banking the board with the feet – the most important aspect of the gybe. The timing of the rig release is not so critical. If you have speed and the water is flat, you can release it early, even before downwind, and let the board carve under its own steam. This gybe is best suited to super-manoeuvrable wave and freestyle boards. Coming out switch foot is a skill that is needed for classic moves like the duck gybe and a host of freestyle tricks. For beginners, it is a purer, less complicated move that gives you less to think about.

On the downside, keeping the board carving with the feet in their original positions and taking control of the sail on the new side demands a big twist at the hips. If you lose speed at the end, with all your weight on the tail, there is a greater chance of sinking and stalling. It becomes increasingly tricky on big boards and in marginal winds.

Training Tips

Success comes as much from organization and planning as it does from slick technique. The following can really make a difference.

The Training Ground

Choppy water and gusty winds give you a jolt and a tug just when you least need it. Ultimately, you will have to learn to compensate, but in the beginning, they are variables you can do without. Flat water and a constant wind will double your success rate.

For the carve gybe, the footstrap must be wide enough to accommodate the whole foot. Only then can you bend the ankle and project the knees and hips into the turn. (John Carter)

The Equipment
You can carve gybe on any modern board that planes. However, the largest boards have features such as long fins, extreme width, and outboard-mounted footstraps that resist turning and a comfortable gybing posture. Boards under 130ltr, meanwhile, are more manoeuvre-orientated. They may be slightly more nervous but they allow you to develop a solid technique that will work on much smaller boards.

Rigs are the same – the big ones are heavier to handle and slower to rotate. A perfect practice day, therefore, with winds of about 17–21kt (force 5), would allow you to use a sail of 6.5sq m or less.

The Set-Up
The set-up that allows you to sail comfortably and fast in a straight line should also be good for gybing. Certain things, however, make all the difference as you carve a turn.

Extreme width forces you to modify your carving position. Ross Williams gybes his 1m (3ft) wide Formula board. (John Carter)

- Make sure the front footstrap accommodates your whole foot. If it is too tight, you will not be able to bend the ankles and project your knees and hips into the turn.
- If you have a choice, mount the front straps on the inboard settings. The closer your front foot is to the centre-line, the more control you have.

Power
If anybody advises you to take out a smaller sail to give you a little more time, be sure to pay absolutely no attention. You have to be fully planing to do a carve gybe! A smaller sail may just allow you to get in the straps, but unless you are skimming right up on top of the water, the edges will sink too deep as you carve and you will stall and trip over.

Keep reminding yourself that speed is your friend. The right amount of power is when the rig drives you on to the plane without much effort. Then when you look down, you see that just the area behind the front footstraps is in contact with the water.

Focus
A good carve gybe lasts no more than five seconds, during which many things happen. Hugely developed though the human brain is, it can only really focus on one thing in that space of time. Given that everything flows out of sufficient speed and preparation, focus first of all on just unhooking, taking the back foot out and so on, without losing speed. Then focus on letting the rig pull you to the inside; after that, think about keeping even pressure on the turning edge and try not to worry about the rig and foot change.

As the carving becomes more automatic, turn your attention to the rig. First, be aware of holding the mast out in front all the time; then think about the back hand moving in and out to keep it powered. As you look to tidy up the rig and foot change, think about the timing of the release and catch and the position of the feet as you change them to keep the board carving.

It is very important to keep changing the focus, otherwise you risk getting into a rut and your gybes will become stale.

A Gybe for all Boards

An experienced windsurfer will hop on any board and rig of any size or design and within a few runs will have adapted his technique to gybe it fluently. The basics of the turn remain the same but there are some differences.

Wide Boards

For 'place the back foot on the inside edge' read, 'take a giant stride to the inside edge'. A board of more than 70cm (27in) set up for blasting or racing has an aggressive set-up with the straps right out on the rails; so when you take the back foot and put it on the inside rail, the legs end up uncomfortably far apart. You physically can't bend both knees into the turn and so have to face more to the front of the board. The front leg will remain pretty straight but this is unavoidable, whilst the back one pressures the rail.

Strange as it seems, you may have to slow down! The big kit is so efficient that in wind speeds of 7–16kt (force 3–4) you may well be travelling faster than the wind itself. As you bear away and overtake the wind, the sail will back (the wind hits it from the wrong side) and you will stop. As you enter, therefore, you may have to head up or sheet out a little to slow down before carving in.

Be patient with the carve. A big wide board will not turn on a sixpence. If you try to hoof it, the thick rails are likely to skip out of the water. Ease gently on the rail and let it follow its own relatively wide arc. Coming out of the turn, the front foot can get caught in the strap, so pull it a little way out before you go into the carve.

You need the rig's power to help you round. Keep the mast upright and aim to sail away clew first before flipping the rig.

Free-Ride Boards

These are the most versatile boards and you can gybe them just about however you like. Some have multiple footstrap settings inboard and outboard that allow you to get further towards the middle of the board and gybe more off the front foot. The trick is to experiment with foot pressure and width of arc to find the board's most comfortable turning circle.

As you take out bigger rigs in the search for speed, the main issue is that of controlling the power and keeping the edge in contact with the water. The technique to develop is that of 'oversheeting', which means pulling in the back hand to the point of stalling the sail and killing some of the power, at the same time leaning heavily on the front hand to get power into the mastfoot and hold the nose down.

Freestyle Boards

The more specialist models – short, flat, fat boards designed to slide around and go backwards – do not carve that well, especially not in chop and at high speeds. The best tactic is to keep the turn tight, slow down and favour the back foot to 'slash' it round.

Wave Boards

These are turning machines. If they feel difficult to gybe, it is because you are being too gentle and not banking them hard enough. Imagine yourself on a surfboard. Get the front foot right through the strap and into the middle of the board then initiate the turn off it, aiming to push all the inside rail into the water right up to the nose logo. You must get right forward – if you fall back and drive off the back foot alone, you will spin right round into wind and flop in before you've had time to hold your breath.

Wave boards need to be brutalized. The harder and steeper you bank them, the better they respond. Cisco Goya cranks it over. (John Carter)

CHAPTER 9

MANOEUVRES

There are those who never tire of the thrill of just blasting along in the footstraps. In 1982, while visiting southern Spain, I met a man in Tarifa. His day's sailing would involve leaving the town beach, sailing the twelve miles across the straits of Gibraltar to the continent of Africa, having a quick drink and then sailing back again. No turns needed. That remained routine until the Moroccan port authorities arrested him on suspicion of smuggling. I made the mistake of following him and quickly concluded that, fun though it was, sailing in a straight line could become a little tedious, not to say dangerous as you disappear over the horizon and away from the sight and sound of friends, family and rescue services. For the majority, the eternal appeal of windsurfing comes from manoeuvring.

From a purely practical point of view, the ability to manoeuvre and turn quickly, tightly and consistently in all winds allows you to sail longer and hold station on enclosed waters. If every change of direction is accompanied by a waterstart, you lose both energy and ground downwind.

However, in terms of pure excitement, no other watercraft changes direction with such style, speed, spontaneity and variety as a windsurfer.

There are countless ways to turn a board but in this chapter I have chosen the three most functional – the duck gybe, the slam gybe and the fast tack. Add these to the standard carve gybe and you have an armoury of moves that will allow you to turn round on any size of board in just about any situation. The other methods, and there are many, contain an unnecessarily flamboyant element, which places them in the freestyle bracket. I will look at some of them in Chapter 12.

THE DUCK GYBE

For me this is the best move in windsurfing, the one that seems to make the very best use of the board and rig. When you get it right, there is a sublime sensation of lightness, speed and efficiency. Although relatively easy compared to the latest tricks, it remains the favourite transition of many of the pros, being both dynamic and fluid. When it was invented in the early eighties, the duck gybe was cast as a freestyle trick to be attempted only by experts until someone discovered that under certain circumstances it can be faster and more effective that the standard carve gybe.

What is it?
The duck gybe is just a standard switch-foot carve gybe with a different rig change. In a carve gybe, you release the back hand and let the end of the boom swing over the nose. In a duck gybe you release the front hand and let the mast swing over the nose, as you 'duck' under the foot of the sail.

In a carve gybe you initiate the rig change after turning downwind on the

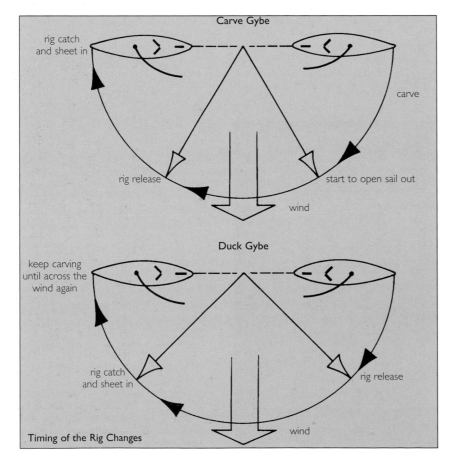

Carve Gybe

rig catch and sheet in

carve

rig release

start to open sail out

wind

Duck Gybe

keep carving until across the wind again

rig catch and sheet in

rig release

wind

Timing of the Rig Changes

new broad reach and sheet in again across the wind. In a duck gybe, it all happens much earlier. You initiate the change before turning through downwind on the original broad reach and sheet in again on the new broad reach.

The photo sequence below makes it look worryingly simple – which it is, so long as you get a few basics right. The following elements make all the difference.

Speed

The faster you go relative to the wind speed, the lighter the rig becomes, and the easier it is to manoeuvre. This is the case in the regular carve gybe and especially relevant in the duck gybe. There is less room for error here, so the more you slow down in the hope of buying a little time, the more the sail powers up and the harder the rig change becomes.

Mobile Hands

Getting from one side of the boom to the other via the clew of the sail is a longer route than in a normal gybe. To make it, your hands have to be mobile on the boom. Many general problems stem from a reluctance to let the boom go. People grab in one place and it takes a crowbar to prise their fingers off. That tension is then transmitted into the rest of the body. As you challenge the more advanced moves, the hands slide all over the boom to get the best leverage, sometimes letting go altogether.

Making Room

The duck gybe seems awkward to begin with, because as you release the front hand, your path to the new side is blocked by the sail with the result that you end up chewing the boom. Getting too close to the rig is an error that affects many manoeuvres. The secret lies in the front hand. As it lets go, it has to cross over the back hand and make it right to the end of the boom. If it gets there, the sail is out of the way and you have both time and space to complete the next phase. If it only gets half-way, the foot of the sail will block you.

Push and Pull

The one aim is to get the new front hand (what was your back hand) on to the new side of the boom in front of the balance point as soon as possible. Once there, you can open the sail and control the power. The key lies in an active and vigorous rig action. Throw the rig at the front of the board as you let it go and then use the old front hand to pull the end of the boom back over your shoulder so the new side of the boom comes into easy reach.

Hold Position

Just as with the carve gybe, you have to hold your carving position and, keeping constant pressure on the inside rail, use active arms to manoeuvre the rig around you. It is when you start bending at the waist and stretching for the new side of the boom that you lose balance. It is all too easy to get distracted by this new rig move but above all, do not forget to keep pressure on the inside edge and carve the board round.

*Wind
Direction*

It starts just like a regular carve gybe. Board and rig are banked over and the back hand, well down the boom, sheets the sail in.

Duck Gybe Sequence *(Dave White)*

On a broad reach, before downwind, the front hand lets go and crosses over the back hand …

Wind
Direction

… to grab the boom right at the end. And still the board carves around.

Ducking under the foot of the sail, you then throw the rig back over your shoulder so the new front hand can grab the front of the new side of the boom in front of the harness lines.

The new back hand takes hold in its normal place. Although only just through the wind, you already have power back in the rig that you can use to keep you on the plane.

The only thing left to do is switch the feet.

Wind
Direction

When to Attempt it
If you are going into regular carve gybes at speed and emerging from most of them dry, albeit without too much speed, then you are ready to try a few ducks. The duck gybe has afforded many their first planing gybe because you get power back in the sail at a time when the regular carve gybe is running out of steam.

Training Tips
The longer the boom, the more cumbersome the duck gybe becomes. For the first attempts, the sail should be no bigger than 6.5sq m. Ultimately, very small sails with their tiny booms are a delight to duck gybe. In the beginning, however, if your sail is less than 5sq m, it suggests that a very strong wind is offering an unwanted control challenge.

The best learning conditions are in winds of 18–27kt (force 5–6) on flat water, which affords more speed and stability.

Common Mistakes
Most problems are associated with the timing of the rig change. The symptoms are quite obvious and often spectacular.

If you release too early, the mast blows straight down to the water, whereupon rig and board stop … but you don't and launch into a swallow dive with half twist.

If you release too late, the wind blows the rig to the outside and the new side of the boom never presents itself. This is the more common failing as people are conditioned to letting the rig go after passing through downwind like they do in the normal carve gybe.

Here are two tips to help you with your timing, one visual and one audio:

1. If the timing is right, the mast falls at about 30 degrees to the inside of the nose.
2. In a normal carve gybe, the rig release happens two seconds after you start carving. In the duck gybe, it happens after just one second.

THE FAST TACK

You learn to tack a board on day one and mentally cross it off the list of things to do. However, as you move into stronger winds riding a smaller board, you will dis-

cover the difference between your first attempts and doing the same thing on something that barely supports your weight on a choppy sea in a 17–21kt (force 5) wind.

The fast or 'carve' tack is less spectacular but more challenging than the carve gybe because you are turning upwind and therefore battling the forces. The rig tugs harder, the board slows right down, is therefore less stable and you have further to move your feet. If you hesitate for a second, down you go.

It is also more practical than the carve gybe because a tack actually gains you ground upwind. You will see at least as many tacks as gybes at all the good wave sailing venues.

The Technique
If you watch an experienced windsurfer tack a big and a small board, you are unlikely to spot any fundamental differences. It is just that the former forgives your fumbling, allows you to take your time, to tread in forbidden places and to commit peccadilloes that would not be tolerated by the smaller board.

Across the wind, prepare by unhooking, stepping both feet forward of their straps on to the upwind side and moving the front hand to the mast, about 30cm (1ft) below the boom.

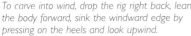

Wind
Direction

To carve into wind, drop the rig right back, lean the body forward, sink the windward edge by pressing on the heels and look upwind.

Coming head to wind, anticipate the drop in sail pressure by leaning forward and inboard. This is definitely not the time to hesitate. Step the front foot in front of the mast …

Planing Tack Sequence (Dave White)

... transfer the mast to the new front hand then in two lightning steps move around the mast.

Wind Direction

As the feet land on the centreline either side of the mastfoot, throw the rig forward.

Angle the rig to windward, sheet in and drive off the front foot to bear the nose away.

As with all the moves to date, initial success comes from focusing on the basics, which in this case are:

- **Speed**. The more speed you carry into wind, the more stable the board is and the easier it is to move your feet.
- **Fast feet**. The quicker you step around the mast and on to the centreline again, the better your chances of survival.
- **Be aware of the volume**. The volume of the small board is concentrated near the centreline and between the mast-foot and the front straps. There is no chance of success if you tread on the nose or the edges.
- **Make room**. By dropping the rig right back as you tack so the clew end of the boom is almost in the water, you open up a clear path around the mast to the new side. As with the gybe, on no account get too close to the rig or it will block your movement.

After a few damp attempts, it is often the small hints and tips that make all the difference.

- **Anticipate**. It only takes one second for a planing small board to carve into wind from across the wind. If you are not beginning to move the feet around the mast after that second, then you are too late and the board will start to sink. It sounds a bit military but you can train yourself in the art by shouting: 'and one and go!'
- **Front foot**. Carve into wind by depressing the rail with the front foot and by swinging the hips and head towards the mastfoot. That way, you are already moving forward in the right direction.
- **Jump or slide**. As a way to get round as quickly as possible, many actually jump the feet in one athletic bound. The more sound technique, however, is to maintain board/foot contact and slide the feet round. The important thing is to make sure the feet are never both in front of the mast at the same time.
- **Feet then rig**. Head to wind, the rig remains angled back, the feet move around the mast and then you throw the rig forward again to bear away on

the new side. If, as many do, you reach for the boom before the feet are round, you will block your path to the new side and end up walking off the nose. Move the feet, then the rig.
- **Look to the front**. Many get half-way round, then spot the new side of the boom and lunge for it, trying to use it as something to hang on to and balance against. However, old gymnastic wisdom decrees that your body follows

your head. So, to get the body and feet to complete the move around the mast, look over your back shoulder as you start to step until you can see the front of the board.
- **Stay centred**. Like so many freestyle tricks, perhaps the best tip for the tack is to concentrate on holding your back straight and keeping the shoulders and hips over the middle of the board as you step round.

Hesitation in moving the feet can lead to this hopeless and potentially injurious situation where you straddle the mast with the feet away from the centreline. The feet have to move simultaneously and swap positions. (Dave White)

Training Tips

The great thing about the small board tack is that the basic technique is the same for all winds, so you can go and practise when the wind is too light or too gusty for enjoyable hooked-in planing. Tactically, many choose to tack when they run into a lull or sense that they are not planing fast enough to carve a good gybe.

Training for tacking is all about finding a rhythm and routine so that the feet and hands automatically move into the right places at the right time, leaving you free to concentrate on timing and balance. This is something that is just as easily done with a board and rig on the beach. Practise stepping round the mast and manoeuvring the rig until the sequence is automatic.

THE SLAM GYBE

This tight, pivoting downwind turn is both fun and functional. Powerful and dynamic, it also produces a crowd-pleasing spray. If done well, the board spins round within its own length. Not only do you lose no ground downwind but, of all the turns, it probably produces the fastest and most spontaneous change of direction. Wave sailors, for example, will often call on it in large surf. Heading out towards a set of waves that are patently too big and powerful to get over, they will throw in a slam gybe to head smartly back to the shore and avoid a rinsing.

Basically, the slam gybe is just a more dynamic version of the flare gybe and is generally performed on small, 'sinky' boards. The 'slam' describes the tail being slammed into the water by the back foot in an explosion of spray to create a pivot. Although often performed in the footstraps in strong winds, this is not a carve. In fact, completely unlike a carve gybe, you deliberately head towards the wind at the start in order to slow down, rather than bearing away to speed up. Like the flare gybe, the turning force comes from the rig, which is scooped to the outside of the turn. The sunken tail creates a minimal surface on which the board can spin like a top.

Key Points

The main challenge of the slam gybe, especially on a small board, is not so much getting the board to turn, but controlling the speed of the spin and getting it to stop.

Slow Down

Many confuse the slam gybe with a tight-radius carve gybe. Hacking across the wind, they lean back, hoof on the tail and are surprised when they explode from the water like breaching whales. At speed, the board is creating so much lift that to kick on the tail sends it bouncing out like a cork. To sink the tail, you need to slow down, and you do that by heading up and sheeting out.

Lean and Commit

Slam gybing is like being on one of those playground roundabouts. Unless you hang on tight, you get flung across the tarmac and into the swings. To counteract the force, you have to drop the body to the inside of the turn right down to water level. An extreme slam gybe looks like a deliberate fall followed by an immediate clew-first waterstart.

Scissor Legs

Although the scooping of the rig initiates the turn, it is by 'scissoring' the legs that you really get the board spinning. As you drop down and sheet in, the front leg kicks the nose downwind; the back leg pulls the tail upwind under your bottom. This is one of the few manoeuvres where you literally kick the board into position. The smaller the board, the easier it is to use the legs in this way.

Unhooked, with the back foot out of the strap and the back hand well down the boom, start the slam gybe by heading up on to a close reach in order to slow down.

Slam Gybe Sequence *(Dave White)*

Initiate the turn by tilting the rig slightly to windward, sheeting in hard and driving off the back foot.

Wind
Direction

The board spins on its tail. Open the sail up almost immediately, switch the feet, and step right forward to halt the rotation. Steady yourself in the clew-first position before flipping the rig.

Stop the Rotation

The board spins round on its tail. To stop the rotation, therefore, you have to get the front section back in the water. Levelling it off comes partly from sheeting out clew first but mainly from switching the feet early and stepping the front foot right up to the mastfoot. Once the front foot is alongside or even in front of the mastfoot, it will be able not only to balance the board but also push the nose off the wind.

Training Tips

Start in sub-planing conditions and work up. The stronger the wind, the faster you turn; the harder the sail tries to fling you to the outside, the more you have to angulate at the hips; the greater the chance of over-rotation then the sharper you have to be. In a wind of about 7–10kt (force 3) you can try it with the feet forward of the straps and get a feel for the trim and the timing.

CHAPTER 10

SEA SAILING

'Jaws' is well known in surfing and windsurfing circles, happily not as the man-eating shark in the Spielberg film but as the biggest and most powerful rideable wave in the world. It breaks perhaps half a dozen times a year off the north coast of the Hawaiian island of Maui. I was there a couple of winters ago watching the formidable action from the cliff.

The power and noise of the wave is awe-inspiring. Windsurfing legend Robby Naish caught a 12m (40ft) monster, somehow just stayed ahead of the pitching 'lip' (the crest of the wave) and made it to the safety of the deep-water channel as literally hundreds of tons of water crashed down behind him. As a regular land-dwelling mammal, it would be reasonable to assume that he either had a death wish or was certified crazy.

An American lady standing next to me reacted to the scene with a mixture of shock and maternal disapproval. 'It's just so ridiculously dangerous … I mean one slip and … well if he's not crushed to death or doesn't drown, who's going to come and get him? It's not fair on the poor rescue services. It's just so irresponsible!' When the venting ceased, I was ready to put the counter-argument but decided that a polite nod in agreement would save a lot of time. Robby and his friends were challenging the limits but as to whether they were being irresponsible? Perhaps not.

On the other hand, a few summers ago I watched a man drag his brand-new board down to my local beach. It was a beautiful day. The sun shone and the flat water was ruffled by a light easterly wind – conditions that might be described as perfect for learning. It was just as well, for this fellow was clearly a newcomer to the sport. It took him the best part of twenty minutes to piece it all together. Shunning all offers of help, he then waddled towards the water (a sizeable belly hung over his garish green board shorts – he was clearly not at his physical peak).

About two hours later, there was a minor commotion as the inshore lifeboat delivered our quivering friend and his equipment back to the slipway where an ambulance was waiting. It transpired that he had finally managed to get going and had already gone some distance out to sea when his outhaul rope came undone. By the time he had managed to sort it out, he had drifted across into the channel between an island and the mainland where an outgoing tidal stream carried him at 4kt straight out to sea. He tried to sail back but being a novice, exhausted and hypothermic (he had no wetsuit) he stood little chance of success. Luckily, he was spotted by a vigilant lady from the sailing club who alerted the coastguard.

So which was potentially the more dangerous situation? Let us examine the facts. Returning to the first scenario, our hero faces waves bigger than hotels. If he falls in the wrong place he could be held down for thirty seconds. His equipment may be destroyed or worse still crash into him and knock him out. But in his favour, he has studied the place thoroughly. He knows where the wave is going to break, where he has to catch it from and which way he has to ride it to reach the safety of deep water. His equipment is the very best, designed specially for the job and he knows how to put it together.

So, what happens if he does make a mistake? He knows how to fall so as to avoid making contact with his equipment. He is also supremely fit, he can swim like a fish and hold his breath for long periods (certain big-wave surfers try to increase their lung capacity and simulate the effects of a big wipe-out by running underwater on the seabed holding rocks). Then, most importantly, if he is in trouble, his buddy is waiting in the channel with a jet ski, ready to dart out in between the waves to fish him out – yes he's brought his own rescue service. Of course, there is still a risk but that risk has been minutely assessed.

In the second scenario, although the conditions were seemingly benign, the novice windsurfer showed how easy it is to find trouble on the open sea if you disregard the rules. Launching into a 3–6kt (force 2) wind on flat water, he was in fact at far more risk than the wave sailor was in 12m (40ft) surf. He had no knowledge of the venue, least of all the state of the tide and direction of the tidal streams. He had not checked his equipment. He was more or less naked in the English sea. He was unfit. He was sailing alone. He had not arranged for somebody onshore to look out for him. Last of all, he wasn't very skilful. It was only going to take a minor change in his circumstances before he found himself literally and metaphorically out of his depth.

COMMON SENSE

The traditional way to approach safety on the sea is with a long and threatening list of hazards, aimed at persuading the eager newcomer that just to dip a toe in the ocean is to court certain disaster. In reality, all it takes is just a modicum of common sense, and the experience of taking your windsurfer to sea will be a totally positive one. You just have to be aware that while rejoicing in the space, freedom, and variety of conditions, not everything lurking around the next bend is friendly.

There are three variable and potentially hazardous factors to consider as you stride to the beach and the deep blue yonder – your equipment, the elements and you.

*'Don't look behind you!' Robby Naish flirting with 'Jaws', to date the biggest rideable wave in the world.
One slip could prove disastrous but the risks have been minutely assessed.*

EQUIPMENT

Equipment failure of some kind is responsible for the vast majority of incidents out to sea. Like modern cars, boards and rigs these days are very solid and reliable. As they are not expected to fail, we tend to overlook inspecting the various components and so take the slightly precarious approach of waiting for them to break before replacing them. So, what is likely to break and what can you do about it?

Mastfeet

The inshore lifeboat at Hayling Island in Hampshire reported recently that 70 per cent of call-outs for windsurfers were due to mastfoot failures – that is, snapped UJs. Try not to be seduced by over-ambitious lifetime guarantees that accompany certain makes. The new materials are incredibly strong but they are all fallible. Subjected to unholy stress plus the degrading effects of sun and salt, they will eventually fail. Check for little tears or stress lines in the rubber. If you sail frequently, consider changing the UJ after eighteen months.

Make sure you have a 'UJ saver'. This is a webbing strap or a thin rope that attaches from the top to the bottom of the mastfoot and holds board and rig together long enough for you to fly the rig and limp home, should the UJ snap. If you don't have a saver or if this snaps as well, then you can take the spare downhaul rope, feed in under the mast base, and tie it back on the mastfoot. Brace your front foot against the base of the mast as you sail gently back to stop it bouncing around and damaging the deck.

Fins

Fins usually break when you run aground, in which case you wade in and get a new one. In rarer cases, smacking a rogue piece of chop, landing askew from a jump or using too big a fin in over-powering winds can cause a sufficiently brutal shock load to blow it away. Sadly, when fins do break (and I stress it is rare), they invariably sheer right at the base so you are left with nothing.

If you have a daggerboard, put it in the 'down' position and, although the back of the board will fishtail, you should have no difficulty in getting back. Just stand well for-

ward of the straps and don't try to plane.

If you are on a smaller board without a daggerboard, there are two accepted ways to get home.

The first is to sail. The tail has no resistance so if you apply any sudden pressure to the back foot, it will slide off downwind. So stand forward on the board with feet either side of the mastfoot. Unhook from the harness and pull on the power very gently. Keep the board going straight through a push-pull action of the feet. If the tail slides away, for example, pull it in with the back foot and push on the front foot. At the same time, create a little sideways resistance by pushing on the heels to sink the windward edge. This can be quite tricky at first. On courses, I often get people to try and sail without a fin as it makes them especially sensitive to foot and rig pressure.

The other way is to use the harness. Take off your harness and fasten it through the back footstrap so the back of the harness lies under the tail. It provides enough drag and resistance to keep the back of the board on track … apparently. Some people, proficient performers, swear by this method. I tried it once and felt as if I was towing a bucket.

Masts

Masts are treacherous, a brand-new one can fail without any apparent provocation. The damage is often invisible – it may have taken a knock in transit that fractured some of the internal fibres. If a new mast is going to break unannounced, it generally does so within the first few minutes of sailing, so stay especially close to shore during the first session.

Masts and indeed all rig components are most at risk if they become caught in a heavy 'shore-break' – the waves that peak and crash on to a steeply shelving beach. While this can turn out to be expensive, at least you will have no problem getting back as you haven't gone anywhere.

If the mast breaks away from the shore, your course of action depends on exactly which section has broken. If it has broken within 1–1.2m (3–4ft) of the tip, you should still have enough sail area to power you home. A tactic on a very small board, which needs more power to keep it afloat,

is to keep the rig flying but to drift across the wind with both feet resting on the board in an 'about-to-waterstart' position.

If the mast has broken within about 0.6m (2ft) of the base, undo the downhaul, remove the mastfoot, discard the broken section and re-rig it. The sail will set like a bag and be horribly unstable, but it will provide enough power to get you back.

If it breaks half-way up by the boom connection, which is the most usual place, then life becomes more difficult. There is, however, a way of re-rigging it. If the broken part is the top half of a two-piece mast, extract the broken half and throw away the shorter section. Invert the other section, feed it via the cut-out back into the luff sleeve and shove the thin end into the unbroken section. You then have enough mast to support a reasonable sail area and get back. Yes, it is as hard as it sounds. I have done it myself. As to whether it is practical – read on!

Booms

Booms can break or bend through old age, as the result of the impact of a catapult or a trouncing in the waves, and sometimes through sheer stress. Preventive measures include checking the rivets and screws that attach the front end, as well as the rope that goes around the clamp. The situation to avoid is sailing over-powered with a big sail with the back end fully extended. The more extended it is, the greater the stress on the boom arms and the ends.

Generally, just one of the boom arms will break or pull out of the front end. If this happens on the way out then you can turn round and still use the good side to get back. If it breaks on the way in then you can either sail back clew first if land is not too far away and you feel like showing off, or you can take the boom off and put it back on upside-down.

With one arm hanging off or missing, the boom will be considerably weaker, so don't sheet in fully, and come back in off the plane.

Boards

Boards have been known to snap in two but rarely without some hefty encouragement – namely landing flat from a high jump. If the board splits right between the footstraps, not much can be done apart from sailing the bigger piece home (the bit with the rig still on it) from the waterstart position.

In normal conditions, the nose may break off as the result of being smacked by a falling boom or running very hard into a steep piece of chop, but you will still be able to sail home.

THE ELEMENTS

Air temperature, the state of the tide and the strength and direction of the wind can combine to produce wonderful, impossible or plain treacherous windsurfing conditions at the same venue.

The problem is that this is a vast subject. Never has there been a better example of a little knowledge being a dangerous thing; but neither is it the case that the more you find about it all, the safer you become. Far more important than stacks of meteorological knowledge is knowing what combinations, in terms of wind direction and state of tide, work best at your chosen coastal venue; and what specific dangers tidal streams, rip currents and hidden obstructions present. Such knowledge is available in the form of a proficient local sailor or the staff of the nearby windsurfing shop. However, that cannot serve as an excuse for me to avoid the issue completely.

Wind Direction
The wind direction determines how easy it is to launch and get going, how safe it is away from the shore, and the size and nature of the waves. Here are the good and bad aspects of each wind direction.

Dead Onshore
If there is no shore-break, you can reach up and down parallel with and near to the shore. If you do have a problem, you will be blown straight in.

However, it can be tricky just getting away from the shore, as you have to sail immediately upwind. Beachstarting is a problem as you cannot bear off to increase the power in the sail – a situation made all the worse if there is any kind of shore-break.

Side Onshore
The advantages of this direction are that you can beachstart across the wind, head out diagonally and hit any shore-break head on. Being onshore, the wind will still blow you back to the beach if you get into trouble.

In most instances, this is the ideal wind direction for general sea sailing.

Side Shore
You launch across the wind and your reaching course takes you straight in and out through any waves and shore-break. Generally, the waves have had less space in which to build up so the sea state is friendlier.

On the downside, if there is a headland, the wind will be sheltered and gusty inshore. Unless you force yourself to turn, you very quickly end up a long way from the beach. As the wind blows parallel with the shore, it could blow you into potentially dangerous territory if you get into trouble.

Offshore Winds
Every traditional safety manual advises windsurfers to avoid offshore winds. The advice is well meaning and founded in sense. If you get into trouble, you could keep drifting on the wind until you hit another shore, which may be part of a different country. Furthermore, obstacles on the foreshore interrupt the wind, making it 'swirly' and gusty by the beach.

You may decide to go further out because the wind gets stronger and more consistent as it clears the shore. But further out, the waves have had space to build. They make you fall more often. Every time you fall, you lose more ground and drift into a stronger wind zone with bigger waves. To get home you have to sail upwind, which is the most testing sailing course. However, you may not be able to because you are already exhausted and the conditions are too severe.

That situation is all too common. However, to issue the blanket statement: 'all offshore winds are lethal, do not go windsurfing!' is misleading to the point of dishonesty. I can name three hugely popular windsurfing venues where the prevailing wind blows from the land – Sotavento in the Canaries, Tarifa in southern Spain and Dahab on the shores of the Red Sea. On any given day, you will see hundreds of windsurfers of all abilities having the time of their lives in fabulous and safe conditions.

At these venues where there are no huge obstructions by the beach, the wind is clear inshore, so you can sail within feet of the water's edge on the flattest water. Consistent wind and smooth water make the very best training grounds. Another factor in warm climates is that the offshore wind, as is the case at Sotavento, may be a thermal. It funnels through the mountains and is actually stronger near the beach, dropping as it blows out to sea.

Although potentially treacherous, offshore winds can offer the best training conditions of all, like here at the Red Sea resort of Dahab.

At the right venue, offshore winds provide the easiest sea sailing conditions. It is not the wind itself that is dangerous, but rather the sailor's lack of preparedness – more about that shortly.

Tide

In the Caribbean, the difference between high and low tide is less than 1m (3ft). In parts of the UK it can be as much as six times greater than that. This has a massive effect on the state of the sea and the venue as a whole. A tide timetable, which tells you the extent of the rise and fall as well as the times of high and low water for each day, is as essential as knowing the strength and direction of the wind.

If, for example, I ring the beach and discover there is an 11–21kt (force 4–5) southerly, which is dead onshore, I know that if the tide is high, waves will be dumping on the steep shingle bank. The waves away from the beach will be confused and tightly spaced, and the breakwaters partially covered. (These are a series of wooden posts dug into the sand to prevent erosion, which stretch about 50m/55yd out from the shore and present a line of impassable barriers to anyone trying to tack out.) Worse still, the wind tends to lift up over the beachhead, leaving a lull right where you try to launch. In short, it's a sight that persuades many to turn round and head straight for the pub.

At low tide, however, the picture is altogether different. The water has retreated beyond the breakwaters. Some 90m (100yd) offshore, a long sandbank emerges, which acts as a natural barrier to the waves. Inshore you are left with a dreamy waist-deep lagoon. The onshore southerly wind allows you to sail all the way along it in the flattest water and practise those carving moves in total tranquillity.

In less than six hours, the difference between high and low tide, windsurfing conditions can change from dire to glorious.

At some venues, at certain states of tide, it may not be possible to sail. There are beaches in the north-west of England where the sea disappears some 16km (10 miles) away at low tide, which is one mighty walk with all your gear. There are other places where the sea floods the entire beach and washes against the sea wall at high tide. Launching and landing become an added challenge.

Before sailing at a new venue I always try to get a look at the place at low tide in order to note the position of obstructions such as rocks, reefs and wrecks that may lurk just beneath the surface, ready to break off your fin.

Tidal Stream

'Tide' describes the rise and fall of the water. 'Tidal stream', meanwhile, describes the horizontal movement of that water as it floods and ebbs. In most places there are two high and two low tides in one 24-hour period and the direction of the tidal stream changes soon after high and low water. However some places have double tides and in others the direction of the stream may not change until one or two hours after high or low water. Local knowledge is once again the key.

Direction
The direction of the stream normally follows the contour of the land and so flows parallel with the shore. If you time it right and the stream is flowing towards the wind, it acts like an upwind conveyor belt. You must be especially vigilant around estuaries and deep-water channels. The tidal stream follows these channels, which often go straight out to sea.

Timing
The tide generally lasts about six hours. At high and low water the stream is slack. It then gradually accelerates and runs at its fastest in the third and fourth hours. If you are at a venue where the tidal stream flows out to sea, the middle hours of an ebbing tide are a good time to be on the shore.

THE HUMAN ELEMENT

You have to be sensible and not launch your 200ltr all-rounder and 6sq m sail into a 34–40kt (force 8) gale and crashing waves. However, if you never dip a toe into uncharted waters, how are you going

Two pictures of West Wittering on the Sussex coast taken at different states of tide. An onshore wind at high tide produces a lumpy sea with mushy rollers rumbling over the treacherous, semi-submerged breakwaters. Just a few hours later at low tide, a sandbank emerges and cuts off the waves to leave a waist-deep, flat-water lagoon – a dreamy 'gybe-atorium' as the locals call it. (John Carter)

To excel on the sea, you have to relish the ocean environment and the prospect of the odd swim. To think of tackling the infamous shore-break here at Brighton beach, you have to be positively in love with it. (John Carter)

to improve? What is essential, is that you are physically and mentally 'up for it' and that your equipment is suitable. Only then have you a chance of learning the extra skills needed to cope with that other variable – waves.

Mental

If you launch on the sea with your finger resting permanently on the panic button and your whole being consumed by the thought of simple survival, nothing good will come of it. To excel on the open sea, you have to be relaxed in the environment and relish the prospect of the odd swim.

Physical

The greatest danger to the newcomer is exhaustion. Until you settle into it, every aspect of your game – sailing along, the extra falls, the waterstarting – is more tiring. So nibble at the challenge by staying close to the shore and going out for short 10–20-minute sessions. Use the rest periods to get your breath back, analyse your performance and observe others.

Equipment

Is control in rough seas all about the skill of the sailor? Ultimately yes, but the best in the world look calm and collected because

they are using boards and rigs that not only match the conditions but also each other.

Matching Board and Rig

Every board will have a recommended sail range. It is when you try to use a rig outside the sail range that it all goes wrong. A typical sight is that of the ambitious improver loading his wide 180ltr board up with a 5sq m sail and taking it out on to a wavy ocean in winds of 17–27kt (force 5–6). The small rig has neither the power nor weight to hold the board down. At speed, the big fin creates too much lift and when this is combined with the bouncing effect of the waves, it will leave him hanging on to a bucking bronco. It will be no surprise if he returns convinced that sea sailing in strong wind is for gorillas only.

However, that 180ltr board can work well on the sea, so long as when the winds are fairly light you use a rig of 6.5–9sq m. In winds of 17–27kt (force 5–6), a sailor weighing 70–80kg (155–176lb) needs a sail of 5.5–4.5sq m. The board to suit that sail range will be less than 100ltr.

THE TECHNIQUES

Some are immediately struck by how

much easier it is to sail on the sea. Having coped with a capricious inland wind that puffed and swirled through the valleys, over the trees and around the hills, they find the constant sea wind a complete joy. With a steady pull in the sail, they can commit to the harness in the knowledge that the wind will not suddenly shut off. They can get up to speed and enjoy longer reaches where they can experiment with foot pressure and body position; they can concentrate on finding the perfect board and sail trim. What makes sea sailing technically more challenging are the waves.

Stance through the Waves

Riding a bicycle over rough ground is easy until you slow down, at which point every bump throws you off balance. It is the same on a board. If you keep your speed up, you skim on the tops of the waves. If you slow down and let the board sink back into the water, the nose butts into the faces and you rise and fall over every lump. Controlled speed is once again your friend.

A good windsurfer makes a rough sea look flat. His upper body is still and relaxed; he holds the rig upright, and keeps it powered up without moving it. In

The only way to get comfortable in rough, windy sea conditions is to get the right tools. This slightly built (60kg/132lb) woman looks calm and collected even in a choppy 22–27kt (force 6) because she has matched her small 4.2sq m rig with an equally tiny 68ltr board. (John Carter)

contrast, his legs are working like pistons, rising and extending again to absorb the waves and maintain board–water contact.

Sailing on the sea forces you to make that transition from passenger to pilot. Rather than just standing there and going along for the ride, you have to assume a more active role in steering, trimming and compensating for the ever-changing terrain.

The waves make the board skip around, so keep constant tension through your legs. Through the smaller chop, think about driving the board on to the water with your legs. To let the pressure off is to lose control. Through the bigger lumps and swells, imagine you are sailing with a ceiling just above your head. Unless you let your knees rise to absorb the wave, you will fly off the top and bump your head.

Tilt and trim the board with the feet so

Control and composure on a lumpy sea comes from lowering the body and keeping tension in the legs to blast the board through the chop. However, your greatest weapon is vision. Look ahead to pick the smoothest route between the lumps. (John Carter)

you always present a flat board to the water. For example, if you are sailing across the waves and one rises up to windward, press on your toes to lift the windward edge and let it pass beneath. A dry ride is a fast ride. If, on the other hand, your feet keep smacking the waves, it is a sign of poor anticipation and trim.

Waves – the Bigger Picture

The most potent of your technical weapons is vision. By looking ahead, you can take in the big picture, steer a line through the troughs and avoid confrontation.

Surface conditions can vary enormously within a sailing area. Right next to the shore for example, the waves may be tightly spaced as they run into shallow water. Over sandbanks or reefs, they may be especially steep and confused. In an

area where the tidal stream runs fastest, you may encounter a wind against tide situation, which produces horribly disordered, standing waves. However, further out in the deeper water where the waves have had time to build and arrange themselves into some kind of order, they roll in smooth, even swells. This is a beautiful sea state. You can ride up, down or along them. You can gybe on to the face and use them to bring you round. You can also bear off down them to help you get planing.

Waterstarting

Ultimately, you can use the waves to your advantage. Initially, however, their influence seems only negative. They immediately wash over the sail and make it heavier to recover. They grab at the cloth and pull it down as you begin to fly it. They shelter the wind at water level and so reduce your lift. This is how to cope:

- Aggression. To get the rig up into the clear wind, you have to swim harder and throw the rig harder and higher into wind.
- Go to the tip. In most situations you should swim to the mast tip and handle the rig from there. You will have better leverage and can push the rig higher. If you push from the middle of the mast, it bends and the tip and leech catch the waves.
- Pump it. As soon as you have any daylight under the sail, work it up and down to force air under it and keep it flying. Then get a hand on the boom and sheet in as soon as possible.

Waves have a habit of washing the board out of position. So get brutal! Use a spare hand or foot to throw or kick the board into position, then immediately get a foot on to stabilize it. Getting up is just the same as on flat water, you just need to be more aware of your timing. The wind will drop as you drop into a trough but then pick up again as the wave lifts you into the clear wind. Lying ready with the rig flying and a foot on the board, look upwind and then time your effort and throw the rig up just as the wave wells from behind and lifts your shoulders.

CHAPTER 11

WAVE RIDING AND JUMPING

WAVE SAILING

Wave sailing is the pinnacle. It is what world champions of all disciplines do when they windsurf for fun. If you are already hooked on planing along in a straight line, can you imagine how many pints of adrenaline and endorphins are going to flood your bloodstream when you do the same thing on a tiny board going at twice the speed down the face of a wave?

Wave sailing is almost as old as the sport itself. For some years it was seen as the sole preserve of the young, bronzed and unfairly gifted. Today, mainly thanks to better equipment, it lies within the grasp of any keen and bold recreational windsurfer.

We have already discussed handling waves but that was in the context of handling an undulating water surface. Wave sailing is quite different. The waves peak and break and you actively seek out their company.

The wave sailor planes out through the waves, dodging some and blasting through others. Some are used as ramps to propel him skywards from where his imagination and natural derring-do run riot. He may decide just to float gracefully on the wind before landing and carrying on. He may choose to throw the board up over his head or drop into a backward or forward loop (a full 360-degree somersault still attached to the board and rig) or maybe even a double.

Having made it out through the waves, he turns round and rediscovers his surfing roots. Catching a wave, he carves a series of long, tight turns right on the wave face. Depending on the direction of the wind and how the wave is breaking, he may ride it downwind facing the wave or or upwind with his back to the wave. The only difference between this and pure surfing is that

he has a rig to lend extra power and speed to the performance.

What it Really Takes

Wave sailing tests you on all fronts. It is physically more demanding, and both the equipment and its tuning are quite different. You must understand how different combinations of winds and waves affect your approach and what you can do. There is the whole question of tactics – you have to continually size up the situation and change course in order to end up in the right place to perform or avoid trouble. There are also the new skills and techniques associated with jumping and riding waves, and handling a very small board in very challenging conditions.

How Good?

Fitness and water confidence are more important than innate skill. To flourish as a

wave sailor you must be comfortable in and under the water. You must also accept that some of the time will be spent swimming after your board, getting pummelled and rinsed by breaking surf. If you get cold sweats at the thought of being held under or finding yourself a few hundred yards offshore without either board or rig, then channel your energies elsewhere.

Equipment

You can learn the basics of jumping and riding on a standard free-ride board, as long as it is not much bigger than 110ltr. But as conditions get wilder and you really start to ride the waves, its lack of spontaneous manoeuvrability will become all too apparent.

The first step might be to a small freestyle or free move board, which make good transition models as they incorpo-

Swimming after your kit is an integral part of wave sailing. Dave White enjoying a brisk dip off the Isle of Wight. (John Carter)

Riding and jumping waves – it doesn't get any better than this. Bjorn Dunkerbeck flies down a watery mountain. (John Carter)

rate many wave board features but are a little faster and earlier to plane. Ultimately, however, you need the real thing.

A true wave board is basically a surfboard with a sail. Every design feature – the rocker line, plan shape, rail profile and fin – is geared around manoeuvrability and ease of handling. The only disadvantages are that it is marginally slower to get going and not as good upwind.

Size

First, let us define the new parameters of size. In the great scheme of things, a 110ltr board will seem minuscule next to the thing you learned on, but to a wave sailor it is huge.

On no account be seduced by the outrageously small boards used by the specialists. A healthy move in recent years has been the development of wave boards as large as 90–100ltr, which can be a huge help to you when trying to survive the lulls and stay planing. Also, in the early stages, you will be sailing in onshore conditions much of the time where you have to sail upwind to burst through the waves and get away from the beach. The bigger the board and fin, the better it goes upwind.

As your fitness and skills improve, you should then move to a smaller board as it is lighter and easier to throw around in the air and allows you to get into more extreme positions on the wave face.

Sails

Most modern free-ride sails work well in the waves. The limiting factor is size. If you take a sail much bigger than 6.5sq m out into surf, you are asking for trouble. A wave breaking on top of a large surface area of cloth exerts so much strain on the extremities of the rig that something has to give, be it the mast, boom or the sail itself.

Aim to take out as small a rig as possible. It is lighter in the hands and easier to throw around in the transitions. The shorter boom allows you to get closer to the wave face, it is quicker to waterstart and the smaller the rig, the less chance it has of breaking.

If you plan to spend a lot of time in the waves, specialist wave sails are a good investment as they are more heavily reinforced in the most vulnerable areas. They

One of the great things about wave sailing is that there is no need for much equipment. One board and three sails allow you to tackle most conditions. Top pro Nik Baker, however, has other ideas. (John Carter)

Wave rigs are capable of putting up with unholy abuse. This one emerged from the washing machine without a scratch. (John Carter)

also have a flatter profile, providing the instant power control essential in critical situations, but this does mean that you sacrifice a little raw power for ease of handling.

The Set-Up

Here lies a major change in emphasis – on a wide free-ride board, you set yourself up for speed, but on a wave board you set yourself up for manoeuvring.

The difference lies in where you direct the power. For speed, the main source of lift and performance is the fin. Therefore, you set the footstraps quite far out on the edge and direct the power laterally against the side of the board and the fin. The fin then transforms that power into lift and forward speed. On the wave board, the feet should be in the middle of the board so you can use both feet to drive the edge and hold the board in the water.

The key to carving and controlling a wave board is to steer off the front foot. By driving off the front foot and leaning down on the boom to apply pressure into the mastfoot, you engage the edge right up to the nose and slice through the water. If you lean on the back foot only, you just pivot round, skip out and lose all your speed.

Front Footstraps

The front footstraps on a wave board are mounted much further inboard, nearer to the centreline. Make sure you open them right up so the toes of the front foot are across the centreline and can apply pressure to the inside edge.

If you wish, you can start to customize your set-up. For example, some boards offer a choice of inner and outer footstrap plugs. On your jumping side going out, you might prefer to use the outer plugs as you are essentially looking for speed and acceleration. However, on the wave-riding side coming in, you want control in the turns and so may favour the inner settings.

Back Footstraps

The back footstraps also have to accommodate the whole foot for control when jumping and riding. Unlike gybing, you wave ride with both feet in the straps. The back foot therefore has to straddle the centreline so it can transfer pressure from edge to edge and re-direct the turns.

As you jump, try to trim the board in such a way that you float on the wind. With the back foot across the board, you can use toe and heel pressure to lift the windward edge and encourage air to blow under it. The fit should be such that every move of the feet and legs has immediate effect. The straps should be open and the feet deep in them but they must still be a tight fit, otherwise you may slip out of them by mistake in mid-manoeuvre. By experimenting with different holes, you can adjust the width and get them to grip the sides of the foot.

The Rig and Stance

The most effective wave sailing stance is upright. The nearer your centre of gravity is to the centreline of the board, the more quickly you can shift weight from edge to edge. An upright stance is also more comfortable when the feet are resting flat in the middle of the board. If you drop down and hike way out to windward, the ankles have to bend uncomfortably. The way to achieve this upright position is to maintain the boom at around shoulder height and just extend the legs.

Many windsurfers, myself included, lengthen their harness lines by a couple of inches when moving from racing (where I use 61cm/24in lines) into waves (where I

The set-up and stance for waves are geared towards manoeuvring and control. The high boom leaves you in an upright, centred stance ready to move the weight upwind or downwind. Longer harness lines give you greater freedom to trim the sail hooked in. The footstraps are mounted right in the middle of the board to allow you to drive it through the turns as if you were surfing. (John Carter)

use 66cm/26in lines). There are three obvious advantages:

1. For early planing with a small sail, longer lines allow you to hold the rig forward as you pump the sail.
2. You spend a lot of time hooked out when wave sailing, notably when riding and negotiating white water. Long lines allow you to hook in comfortably in or out of the footstraps and take a well-earned rest.
3. For moves like hooked-in jumps, long lines put a little distance between rig and body, giving you more time and space to adjust the power in a crisis.

Common Failings

As people make the transition to a wave board, two things tend to hinder their progress. The first is that they rely on the power in the sail and fin to get them going, the second is a general passivity.

The short, swept-back wave fin is designed primarily to hold the board in through fast, steeply banked turns. It has neither the area nor the profile to resist heavy sideways forces. If you just hook in, sheet in and drive against the fin at slow speed, as you might on a bigger board, it will slip sideways and stall.

To get a wave board planing, do not rely on the fin. Instead, bear away more to increase the drive in the sail. Then, when you are planing, you can drive off it and use it to take you upwind.

You are unlikely to get much out of a wave board and rig if you just stand there and wait for something to happen. You have to be active. The wind is gusty around the waves, so keep working the rig, pumping it sharply with the back hand until you get fully planing. At the same time, stay on your toes and be especially aware of the trim. The wave board takes every change in foot pressure as a command to turn. As you get into the straps and then sail along in a straight line, concentrate on holding it flat and level.

Understanding the Conditions

When they realize that wind and waves can combine in a multitude of ways to produce classic, dreadful or plain dangerous conditions, wave sailors very quickly become amateur oceanographers and meteorologists.

The main elements to recognize are how, why and where waves break, and how the wind direction affects not only the shape and form of the waves but also what you can do with them.

Waves

Waves, seismic eruptions notwithstanding, roll up the shore as either wind waves or groundswell. Although we aspire to ride the latter, usually we must make do with the former.

Wind Waves

As the name suggests, wind waves are formed as a direct result of the wind disturbing the water surface. They start their life as 'chop' (small, irregular lumps moving out from the source of the wind), deepening and lengthening as they roll along. However, even if they are big, wind waves are characteristically messy, irregular, tightly spaced and relentless. Being wind-driven, as soon as they start to peak, the wind blows the crests down, making them break prematurely and leaving the sea looking like a boiling cauldron of rumbling white water.

Groundswell

These are the beautiful, clean waves that adorn the surfing posters. They are basically wind waves with a bit more history.

Wind waves travel at varying speeds; so as they move away from the source of the wind, they begin to catch each other up and merge until eventually they form into long, well-defined lines. These swell lines roll up in groups or 'sets', often of three or five, but it can be just about any number.

One of the beauties of sailing or surfing in groundswell is that there is a calm period between the sets, enabling you to make your way out. The longer the time between the sets, the further you are from the source of the swell.

Swell can roll across an entire ocean, ending up thousands of miles away from the cyclone that created it, which is why huge waves can roll up on the shore on a windless day. Surfers and windsurfers in search of good waves, check the forecasts for places many miles away from their chosen beach. Hawaiians, for example, monitor the typhoons in the north Pacific off the coast of Japan. Meanwhile, Cornish, Welsh and Irish wave sailors look for storm activity in the distant Atlantic off

Newfoundland to produce their waves.

The Break

Something has to generate the waves but something also has to make them break. Wind waves or swell may be hitting a whole stretch of coastline but actually only peaking and breaking at just a few spots. Such spots are called 'breaks'.

Waves break when something trips them up in the form of an underwater obstruction like a reef, a sandbank or even a gradually shelving seabed. An unbroken wave is no more than a pulse of energy – the water itself is not moving. At this stage it is relatively long and shallow. When it moves into shallow water that energy is squeezed, which causes the wave to jack up and become shorter but steeper.

The wave breaks when the top overtakes the base. Friction through coming into contact with the seabed slows the bottom of the wave. The top continues at the same pace and topples over, turning into a moving wall of foaming water.

How the wave breaks, whether it is mellow or powerful, depends on the size of the swell and how suddenly that energy is squeezed. Here are two extreme examples.

Waves whipped up by the local wind (wind waves) will roll up in irregular lumps. While there is fun to be had from riding and jumping them, there is no order to the sea, which looks like a boiling cauldron.

This is a sight to make the wave sailor salivate. A beautiful, clean groundswell, the product of a gale in the North Atlantic, marches into southwest Ireland in sets of four of five waves. It is not a product of the local wind, which, from the spray blowing off the crests, you can tell is slightly offshore. (John Carter)

Off the Hawaiian Islands, swells roll in from the north and west through some of deepest ocean trenches in the world, 7,000m (20,000ft) in parts. Having no contact with the ocean floor, they travel very fast. They then run into the reefs that protect the islands. On the famous surfing and windsurfing beaches these may lie as little as 1.8m (6ft) below the surface. The energy is squeezed so suddenly that the wave immediately doubles in height. It is then that the crest throws over so violently that it forms a hollow tube or barrel shape and crashes over with awesome power.

The same swell rolling up a shallow shelving beach will heap up and break more gently because much of the speed and energy is sapped as it gradually makes contact with the seabed. Without that sudden change of depth, the crest does not so much throw over as crumble impotently.

Waves for Windsurfing

The perfect wave – long and well-defined, peaking in one spot and then peeling either left or right – is as rare as the proverbial blue moon. However, you at least want a wave with the odd steep section that holds up for long enough to give you time to work a few turns before breaking. The worst situation is where the wave 'closes out', that is to say, it peaks and crashes suddenly along its whole length. It's good for munching gear and little else.

For jumping, any wave will do so long as it has a steep face. A big, beautifully clean, peaking groundswell makes for a classic jumping ramp, but weak, messy wind waves are arguably preferable. There are more of them and if you bail out and fall, they lack the power to inflict much damage as you swim around trying to get started again.

Pozo, on the island of Grand Canaria, is the jumping capital of the world. Here, the waves are mostly small and wind blown but it's not unusual to see locals such as Jonas Ceballos flying 15m (50ft) in the air. For jumping at least, a consistently strong wind blowing from the right direction is more important than big waves.

Violent storms in the north Pacific produce the groundswell but it is the shape of the seabed that squeezes that energy and forms the monstrous waves off Maui's north shore. Moreover, because the swell has hit the reef at a slight angle, this wave is breaking in one spot before peeling – perfect for riding … so long as you can hold your breath for at least a minute. (John Carter)

Wind Direction

The direction of the wind determines both the angle from which you approach the wave and what moves are possible both in terms of riding and jumping.

Dead Onshore

A wind blowing straight on to the beach does not bring an immediate smile to the wave sailor's face. The options are a little limited. Reaching parallel to the waves you have to head right up into wind to meet them head on, which makes jumping and the simple act of getting out a little awkward. However, it is a good direction for learning to ride with your back to the wave.

Side Onshore

This is the classic jumping direction in that you reach out diagonally towards the waves and meet them more or less head on at full speed. Furthermore, a wind blowing in from the sea is usually solid right up to the beach so you have the power to get planing straight away and arrive at the impact zone at speed in the straps.

Your natural reaching course back in takes you upwind along the wave face with your back to it. Riding downwind facing the wave is possible but requires some skill as you have to hold the sail clew-first for most of the ride.

Side Shore

This is the classic and all too infrequent direction. When the wind blows across the waves, you have the most options in terms of jumping and riding. So long as the wind is clear inshore, you hit the waves dead on. Then on the way back in you have the option of riding either up or downwind.

Side Offshore

This is the dream direction for wave riding but jumping can be a bit of nightmare. The wind squeezes up the wave to give you a huge gust on take-off but then disappears completely behind it so you land in a hole. On the way back in, you find yourself naturally reaching along facing the wave. Front side downwind riding is the ultimate thrill.

Being offshore, the wind has had no time to create any chop so the waves tend to be smooth and clean.

Direct Offshore

There is not much to be done in a direct offshore wind. It is very difficult to get out and jumping is nigh impossible (you have to take-off on a run). If you can generate

The fierce side-onshore winds at Pozo in Grand Canaria make for ideal jumping conditions.
(John Carter)

A side-shore wind, when it combines with a good swell, gives the most varied riding and jumping options. However, when it is this strong (34–40kt/force 8) it does tend to make the waves break irregularly. (John Carter)

enough upwind speed to catch the wave, riding can be fun but with the wave carrying you into wind, you can suddenly find yourself over-powered.

Wind Strength

At spots where the sea is neither deep nor wide enough to get a groundswell, you need a strong local wind to generate decent waves. Although many associate waves with gales, generally you don't want that much force, especially for riding. Strong winds, especially if they are a little onshore, make for a wildly choppy and confused sea state, as well as blowing the crests over and making them break prematurely. About 17–27kt (force 5–6) is ideal, although some of my most memorable wave riding days have been in as lit-

tle as 7–10kt (force 3). You wobble out through the break off the plane but then, like pure surfing, get picked up on the way back in and delight in shredding an unruffled wave face with total control.

Rip Currents

When a wave breaks, the water surges up the beach before going back the way it came. However, on days when the waves are big or relentless, a new wave may already be pushing up before the old one has had time to suck back, leaving a build up of water at the top of the beach. A rip current is formed as this water seeks alternative routes back out to sea. Generally, it flows parallel to the beach and out along the headlands. Some of it may divert through deeper water

channels where the waves are not breaking.

On big wave days, these rips can be like fast-flowing rivers, the movement of surface water creating standing waves. A smart surfer is always aware of them and will often use one as a free escalator to ride out through the break. As wave sailors we are generally unaffected – unless the wind drops or we get separated from our equipment.

A short time ago, I was sailing in big waves off the Isle of Wight. My board and rig got washed in towards the beach where the rip dragged them off around the cliffs. It was more than half an hour before the rip dissipated and I managed to catch up with them, floating amongst the rocks some half a mile away.

Side offshore is the classic wind direction for wave riding because you naturally ride the wave 'down the line' (facing it). John Skye sets up to bear away down this clean swell on the Scottish island of Tiree. (John Carter)

Wind
Direction

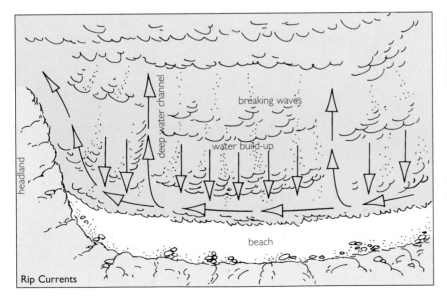

breaking waves

deep water channel

water build-up

headland

beach

Rip Currents

TOP TIP
To get out of a rip, swim across the stream into the still water on either side. It is fruitless to try to battle against it.

Through the Shore-Break

Wave sailing is indeed the best ride at the fair – if you can make it out there in the first place. Launching through the shore-break is a skill in itself. When waves run up a steeply shelving beach, they tend to peak and crash on to the sand or shingle with untold ferocity. At a famous world cup event in Brighton in 1995, the beach's notorious shore-break destroyed no less than thirty masts over the week. It was carnage.

Of course not every beach creates such destructive 'dumpers', but it only takes a relatively small wave to inflict disproportionate damage. Here's a plan.

Avoidance and Timing

Avoid the issue altogether. Check out the whole beach and you will usually find a corner where the shore-break is gentler. Then take a moment to survey the pattern of the waves. There are inevitably short lulls where it suddenly goes flat – this is when to make your move.

Speed and Commitment

When you decide to go, you have to charge without a hint of pussyfooting. You only have to get on your board and sail about 18m (20yd) to make it beyond the trouble zone. As soon as you drop the board in the water, jump on, sheet in and go. Just a moment's hesitation gives the waves a chance to wash the board off line.

Technique

It is absolutely essential to keep both board and rig clear of the water. If, for example, the end of the boom catches a wave, the push and pull of the undertow can rip it out of your hands and the game is over before it has begun.

Stand in knee- to waist-deep water, let a wave wash through you then launch immediately on to the back of it where the water is deeper and try to get away before it starts to suck back. Launching right in front of a wave, where the water is sucking up almost dry, is an act of wilful damage.

When It All Goes Wrong

If you are washed back or drop your rig in or around the shore-break, action has to be dynamic and immediate if you are to prevent injury to both your wallet and yourself.

Forget the board and sprint straight to the tip of the mast, and, as per the water-start, run it round into wind to get air under it and fly it. Your first priority must be to get the rig clear of the water. If you can hold it above the waves, it is relatively safe. Unless the waves are very weak, make a swift tactical withdrawal, drag your kit back up the beach, gather yourself, and try again.

The following are general preservation tips for survival in breaking waves that apply whether you are in the shore-break or further out.

- To avoid having your equipment pummelled into your face, do not put yourself on the shore side of it.

The trick of getting off the beach is to launch onto the back of a breaking wave. (Dave White)

Waterstarting in breaking waves is not always a joy. The trick is to hold the rig as high as possible above the foam. (John Carter)

If you are taken down in the break zone, unless the waves are very big, avoid having to swim after your kit by obeying the cardinal rule of hanging on to something. (John Carter)

- The power of the wave is in the top, so if one is about to break on your rig, grab it and sink it as deep as you can. The wave will then just wash over it.
- It is when the tip of the mast becomes stuck in the seabed that the rig is most vulnerable, as the force of the next wave is liable to concertina it. If you have time, swim the rig so the mast is pointing out to sea, sink it deep and hang on. Eventually you will get washed in, away from the break zone and have time to waterstart. So long as the waves are a reasonable size and you are on the ocean side of your equipment, hanging on to something will save you hours of swimming.

Over the White Water

An unbroken wave is relatively easy to negotiate. As the water is still, you can just pull up your knees and let it undulate beneath you. White water, on the other hand, has two characteristics that make it specially challenging.

Firstly, white water is 90 per cent air. It bubbles and boils, is highly unstable and does not support the board like normal water. Secondly, because it is moving, as you hit white water, it can literally whip your feet from under you. The board stops but you keep going and pile over the front. Also, the rig can suddenly power up, which again leads to a catapult.

Every situation is different but these are the main points to follow:

- Hit it nose first so as to present the minimum amount of board to the white water. If it does catch the rails, it will spin the board round and whisk you on an involuntary ride back to shore.

- Pump the sail for speed so you have enough momentum to carry you over. However, be ready to sheet out as you hit and rise over it.
- Get the weight forward. Ease on to the back foot to help the nose rise over it but then immediately get the weight forward. The tail is the thinnest section, so if you keep standing on it, it will sink down into the foam.

- Because the white water offers so little resistance, the fin has a hard time gripping. As you sail through it, ease off the back foot and come more upright over the board to avoid a spin out.
- If you are planing towards a really heavy barrage of white water, try to pre-jump it, that is to say, pop the board out of the water just before it reaches you so that you land on top of it. Of course, this does rather presume that you know how to jump!

JUMPING

Jumping, and therefore wave sailing in general, gets put on hold by otherwise determined windsurfers because it involves going up and therefore coming down from an unknown height with an unknown force.

As your fin leaves the water for the first time, you enter an alien space where the board suddenly behaves differently and appears subject to a new set of steering and control laws. Technically, however, it

Bursting over white water demands both subtle trim and tenacity. Generate as much speed as possible and then try to pre-jump the hurdle so the nose lifts up and you end up on top of the barrage. Keep the board level. Because the foamy stuff is 90 per cent air, if you weight the back foot suddenly, the tail will disappear. (John Carter)

Controlled flight comes from pulling the board and rig tight into the body, staying compact and not closing your eyes. (John Carter)

Approach the ramp crouched like a cat ready to spring. Then as the tail leaves the lip, extend the legs, spring up off the toes and sheet in.

Drop right down to windward, tilt the rig over your head, tighten your stomach and pull the tail up under your bottom to the same level as the nose. The board is level so the wind can blow under and support it.

By pulling the tail upwind, you should land just off the wind. Bend the knees to absorb the shock.

Jumping Sequence *(John Carter)*

is infinitely easier than the carve gybe. There is no sudden change of direction or rig flip. Once in the air, water, with its random and unsettling chops and lumps, is taken out of the equation and the board is immediately easier to control. Air offers comparatively little resistance so you can push and pull the board into line with minimum effort.

It is certainly a little scary at first; but is it dangerous? Unless you start doing multiple rotations from 12m (40ft) up, it is no more chancy than cranking at full speed across choppy water

Seats for Take-Off

As you get planing, work your feet right into the straps. However much your better instincts are telling you to be prepared to bail out, the very last thing you want is for one foot to slip out by mistake.

Once up to speed and hooked in, you scan the ocean for a likely ramp. A perfect 0.6m (2ft) wall is peaking some 45m (50yd) ahead. Unhook, hang away from the rig, keep the power on and the speed up. Bend the knees in preparation to spring. The slightly onshore wind means you are approaching the wave diagonally, so at the last moment, steer upwind and smack it straight on.

As you climb the face, lift up on the boom and throw the rig forward to help the nose project upwards. Almost simultaneously, sheet in hard and extend the legs so you literally jump off the lip.

Whatever happens next, you will soon be down again, but to make sure you touch down with style, speed and stability, you have to take control of your trajectory. You must drop the shoulders back and pull the rig towards you so the mast is tilted over to windward. Pull the tail right up and under your bottom to bring it up to the height of the nose and to bear away. Look around the mast and spot your landing point, which should lie just downwind of the nose.

A full one and a half seconds later you are preparing for landing. Extend the back leg so the tail makes contact first. At the same time, extend the rig forward again so you land in your sailing position with the sail powering the nose down and forward. Even within the short span of that

introductory jump, a lot is going on. Let me add some flesh to the bones of the essential stages.

Approach and Take-Off

From the outset, take an active approach to jumping. Trepidation leads most people to do the opposite. They believe that the very act of meeting a wave at speed will send them higher than they will ever want to go. However, if you adopt the passive role – holding your stance, closing your eyes and just sailing off the lip – you will not so much jump as flop into the chasm below.

Liken it to high jumping. If you stand there and just fold your legs, you will drop. To get over the bar, you must bend, extend, leap and then pull up your legs up to clear the obstacle.

> **TOP TIP**
>
> To get properly airborne, spring as high as you can and then pull the board up to your level.

Another crucial aspect to jumping, which you would automatically do on dry land, is to take-off on your toes because this is where the spring comes from. As you climb the face, you have to get from the back seat to the front. Lean on your heels to steer upwind and meet the wave head on; but as you climb the face come forward and inboard, transferring your weight to your toes. Then, as you extend your legs, you will go upwards and not just lunge to windward.

Another reason to take-off on your toes (and have the straps inboard) is to lift the windward edge so wind can blow under the board and do much of the lifting for you. Once the windward rail drops, the wind catches the top of the deck and drives it back down.

Getting the 'Pop'

An explosive lift-off comes from timing your leg and extension with a mighty pump of the sail. Just before the tail leaves the top of the wave, sheet in hard. Direct that pulse of power through bent legs into the board. The tail sinks a little, then as it corks to the surface everything projects

up. Extend the legs, pull up and forward on the rig and then pull the tail up. Getting a clean take-off and good height is much more about timing than strength.

Landing

Initially, it is best to go for long jumps where the board is level through most of its trajectory and where you land on the plane. It is also the most tactical jump as it allows you to make swift progress out through the break.

To touch down with speed and avoid a stall or spin out, two things have to happen.

1. You must steer the board in the air with your feet to land off the wind. You will then touch down with the weight on the front foot and the wind slightly from behind, giving you instant forward drive.
2. The back foot should be tucked under the backside so your weight acts downwards on the board and does not deliver a shock load against the fin.

If you find yourself dropping like a stone from any height, the impact of a flat landing can shatter your board, joints and confidence. To ease the blow, extend the back leg to drop tail first. The tail then sinks with an impact-absorbing 'sploosh' rather than an ankle-tweaking 'thwack'.

Higher

With repetition comes a certain familiarity and a desire to scrape the heavens. The first progression in this direction is to head for a steeper ramp with more speed, an act that forces you to develop a new technique – that of soaring.

Soaring

'Soaring' may be a slightly overstated description of those first hops. However, in every jump, regardless of the height, there should be a moment when good technique allows you to hang on the wind.

• Make the board aerodynamic. Not only lift the windward edge but also tuck the back foot right up so the board is level nose to tail – the higher you can lift the tail, the more the board seems to float.

Robby Naish soaring like an albatross some 9m (30ft) above Sprecklesville in Maui. His horizontal rig is acting like a wing, he's controlling his trajectory with his legs and looking down to spot the runway. (John Carter)

Landing with the board flat from any height comes with a health warning but especially when you are plummeting 9m (30ft) out of the Hawaiian sky. So, drop tail first by easing the back hand and extending the back leg. (John Carter)

- Turn the rig into a wing. Think about pulling the rig down to windward (the higher the jump, the more you pull it down), which directs the power upwards.
- Tuck up. The wind can blow you out of shape so make yourself compact.

Problems

When reaching new altitudes, defective jumpers hit the panic button and make like a stranded starfish. They extend their legs in an effort to keep the board in contact with the water and straighten their arms to keep the boom away from their teeth.

With board and rig dangling on extended limbs, which are themselves attached to a jelly body, you are a hopeless and helpless passenger. As soon as you relax your stomach muscles, you lose tension in the core of your body; upper and lower body then sway all over the place making balance and control impossible.

Most of the problems are mental. To jump high, you must really want to do so,

but unless you were born bereft of the self-preservation gene, you just have to chip away at the task. With improved control comes more confidence and with confidence comes the desire to push the envelope.

Aerial Expression

With even as little as 2m (6ft) between your board and the ocean, there is ample opportunity for self-expression. The first step may be to experiment with jumping hooked in the harness. It forces you into a good compact position and also gives you the freedom to take a hand off the boom in mid-air as a gesture of pure nonchalance.

From there the obvious progression is to a 'table top' – a jump where you kick the board to windward and then invert it over your head so the underside faces the sky. The rig is parallel with the ground with the board projected above it.

To get into that position, you need a vertical wave. As you climb, the board itself becomes vertical whilst both you and the rig end up horizontal. You are then in perfect shape to invert the board. You need to decide in advance to do a table top because the inversion must begin the

moment you leave the water. As soon as you have taken off, start to sheet out, drop the body downwind under the boom and push the feet and board upwind and towards the heavens – a move that demands extreme angulation between upper and lower body.

To ensure a successful landing, the board has to be tweaked before you reach the top of the jump because you have to start to bring it back underneath you before you begin to drop.

Loops

You may not believe this but looping is not actually that difficult, although it is certainly true to say that the way certain pros pop them off flat water and continue planing without wetting a single hair, or control the rotation from 12m (40ft) in the air, takes some skill. However, there are many cases of people performing loops within a year of learning to windsurf. Iballa and Daida Moreno, the supremely talented twins from Grand Canaria, could both loop before they could gybe. In fact, Daida claims to this day that she finds gybing more difficult than looping.

Loops are a lot of fun but they have been known to cause some nasty injuries.

A classic no-jump. Sheeted out, legs straight, body over the board – the mind was willing but the body had other ideas! (John Carter)

As you speed towards a lofty vertical ramp, it may be a bit late to ask yourself whether you really wanted to jump high or whether you just liked the idea! (John Carter)

However, as long as you hang on and keep to a sensible altitude, it is far less precarious than it seems.

Back Loop

The back loop is easier to initiate and go for than the front loop but much harder to land. The ideal situation is to hit a vertical

Nik Baker in mid back loop. The key tip for initiating the rotation and staying oriented, is to look over the front shoulder to spot the landing. (John Carter)

ramp of 1.2–1.5m (4–5ft) just before it breaks so it sends you straight up. Do not, on any account, try to initiate the rotation on take-off but go for height. At the top of the jump, sheet out, drop right back over the tail and, most important of all, look back over your front shoulder to spot the landing. That alone is enough to start the rotation. You will come down nose first and the aim is to land virtually downwind.

How easy that sounds! It is a beautiful, slow rotation and success comes from getting a feel for where you are through practice and then controlling the speed of the rotation by sheeting in to go faster or out to go slower.

It is wise to start with back loops because mentally they seem kinder. All the way through the move, you are aware of being upwind of your kit, able to eject it downwind at any time and bail out. That is not the case with the forward loop.

Forward Loop

I did my first forward loop by accident. I was at a speed sailing competition in Fuerteventura. Half-way down the 500m (550yd) course, doing about 35kt, my front foot caught a bit of chop. The board stopped, the sail powered up and I was hurled, still hooked in, into the mother of all catapults. Luckily, my feet were wedged so tightly in the straps that they stayed in position and I took the tiny 38cm (15in)

wide speed board with me. I smacked the water and when I surfaced, I was still hooked in with my feet in the straps facing the same way. I had done a complete 360-degree rotation and hosted an immediate celebration.

So, whenever anyone asks me what the mechanics of the forward loop are, I say, in all good faith, that it is simply a deliberate catapult (or non-deliberate in my case).

The front loop has many variations but the good thing is that you can start low and work up. In the 'speed' or 'spin' loop the rotation is lateral (the board remains more or less horizontal) so it can be done off a 15cm (6in) piece of chop or even flat water. You never need to be more than 0.9–1.2m (3–4ft) off the water. From there you can take it higher and make the rotation more vertical until you are ultimately performing 'end over end' loops where you revolve right over the mast tip.

The sequence of the basic forward loop is quite straightforward. You bear away (the broader you go, the less far you have to spin), unhook, place the back hand far back on the boom and pop a small jump. When the fin has left the water, you must be sure to:

- Throw the front hand forward and sheet in really hard with the back hand to pull the clew through the wind.
- Look round over your back shoulder –

The 'in car' camera view of Robby Naish dipping into a forward loop. See how far the back hand is down the boom.

Mental Warfare

The challenge of a forward loop is 90 per cent psychological and 10 per cent technical. You cannot approach it worrying about the prospect of the casualty unit and potential mortgage payment default. If you really want to do it, then there has to be something that forces you to pull the trigger. Here are some suggestions:

- When somebody else does one, immediately follow suit.
- Do it as part of a group. Go out one at a time while the others watch and perhaps video the action. The ignominy of not going for it with friends watching is often too much to bear.
- Use an oral trigger. Try shouting to yourself: 'jump, look, pull'.
- It can help to do little jumps off the wind and then tweak the back hand to get a feeling of the rig powering the nose down.
- A helmet can be a useful psychological crutch. It also protects the ears (landing on the side of the head can result in burst eardrums). Lightweight padded vests, which protect the ribs and back, may also prove helpful.

As most loopers will testify, once you have at least gone for one and survived, the mental barrier is broken and the floodgates open.

WAVE RIDING

For me, nothing matches the pure joy of riding a wave. It doesn't irritate my already irritable knees as much as jumping and it lasts a lot longer. There is so much to recommend it but the fundamental attractions are the feelings of effortlessness and of tapping into a force much bigger than you. The speed and sensation are second to none.

The Basics

At first, although you may have watched the action live and studied the DVDs, your head will fill with a torrent of unanswered questions. Where do I catch the wave? How do I catch the wave? Which part of the wave do I ride? What should I do and where do I go when I have caught it? Much

where you look is where you end up.
- Pull your back foot right under your backside so you feel as if you are tripping over the downwind edge.

Hold that position and the rig will power you round. In low-level loops, the feeling is that of rolling around the front shoulder and doing a sort of lateral cartwheel over the nose.

Initially, you will probably land on your back in the waterstart position so throw the rig forward immediately to keep going.

Bailing! There is always the option of pulling the ripcord and bailing out. Just make sure you throw your equipment downwind of you so you don't meet it again on the way down. The author in free-fall off Hookipa in Maui. (John Carter)

will fall into place if you grasp a few basic principles.

Where to Ride

Ideally, you 'take-off' (catch the wave) on the peak, that is to say where it is first about to break. You then look to see where it is going to peel and head towards it so you are staying on the unbroken face just ahead of the white water, where the wave is steepest and fastest. Your direction along the wave is often decided by the wind direction (see page 137).

In practice, the wave is likely to be wind blown and therefore messy, irregular, and peeling everywhere and nowhere. However, two key elements apply to all situations.

1. **Sail along the wave**. Easily the commonest error made by beginners is to catch the wave, drop straight down it, and end up miles in front wondering where it has gone. As soon as you catch it, you must make a turn either upwind or downwind back towards the wave so you remain on the face rather than overtaking it.

2. **Seek the unbroken section**. The wave may not be peeling smoothly but seek out an unbroken part nonetheless. You can ride along on the white water – in fact it can be quite a good way to start – but there is not much you can do on it except get pushed to the beach.

When to Stop

It all depends on the venue. At a beach break where the wave gradually loses its power as it runs into shallow water, you can take it all the way to the shore, turn round and beachstart away again. Alternatively, you can gybe out in front of it so you have completed the turn by the time you meet it again. In more challenging conditions, the smart tactic is to kick off the back of the wave just before it collapses. You can then turn round, fairly safe in the knowledge that you will not be confronted by white water on the way back out.

Catching Waves

If there is plenty of wind, catching a wave on a windsurfer is childishly simple. Head slowly upwind, let it catch you up and as it wells up behind you, bear away and accelerate down the face.

If the wind is lighter, you must try to get your speed up to that of the wave by pumping hard. Get the weight forward to force the nose down the face of the wave before slipping back into the straps as you

The primary objectives are to ride along the wave rather than just dropping vertically down it, and to perform your turns on the unbroken face. (John Carter)

accelerate. If the wind is light, and some of the best wave riding is done in sub-planing winds, you have to wait until the wave is just about to break and moving at its fastest before catching it.

So many people bemoan the fact that they are confronted by wave after wave on the way out but can find nothing to ride on the way back in. If the waves won't find you, then clearly you must find them. Without wishing to sound like some spaced-out hippie, the problem may be that you are out of sync with the ocean and need to take the time to get back in rhythm with it, becoming more aware of the cadence of the waves and the gaps between the sets.

Also, any experienced wave sailor will tell you how important it is to keep an eye on what is happening out to sea in order to gauge the state of play, plan your route and catch the wave. So, the next time you make it out there, turn round and be prepared to wait. Stall the board and head gently upwind off the plane until you see the waves welling up on the horizon.

Orientation
It only takes a couple of falls or a tidal stream to take you some distance off course. If a sandbank or a reef is kicking up the waves, there is no point in sailing in the deep water 200m (220yd) upwind or downwind of it. When you first get into the waves, look back to shore and find some point of reference so you always know where you are relative to both the waves and the land.

Catching the wave in the wrong place can be potentially life threatening. Sailors of very big waves line up with a transit on the land so they know exactly where to take-off each time.

Back Side Riding
Choosing side-shore or side-onshore winds, the easiest introduction is to ride the wave upwind with your back to it. Riding upwind, you have better control of your speed, the sail is not so powered and if the wave does take you down, you are on the ocean side of your kit and will not be injured by it.

To begin with, just enjoy the ride. Lean

Riding with your back to the wave is the easier option first off. Having got used to making shallow edge-to-edge turns on the face, start to use the wave. At the top, drop the shoulders into the trough, lean on the toes, bear the underside to the white water and let it push you around and down. (John Carter)

on your heels to carve towards the wave, then level it out and head straight along it to get used to the feeling of being pushed along.

Next, try a little edge-to-edge steering on the wave. Depress the heels to do a 'bottom turn' (a turn at the bottom of the wave) and then use toe pressure to bank

A totally committed, lay-down back side top turn. At the top of the wave with the board almost into wind, drop the rig into the trough, push on the back hand to back-wind the sail and then use that as a lever to drive off the tail and slash the board around. (John Carter)

over the other way to 'top turn' (a turn at the top of the wave). Loosen up and use the hips to move the weight from edge to edge.

Make more aggressive turns and begin to use the power of the wave to redirect the board. Keep looking along the wave for a section that is about to break. Carve into the wave on the heels but then rock over on to the toes to drive in the opposite edge, bear the underside of the board to the white water and let it push you around. From now on, anticipation is the name of the game. When you let the wave smack the board round, the change of direction and acceleration are so sudden that you risk having the carpet pulled from under your feet and falling out of the back door. Whichever way you are turning, anticipate the change by moving the body first. You change direction first – the board follows.

Back side riding is not just for beginners. Some professionals, such as Josh Angulo from Hawaii, have made it something of a speciality. In the huge waves and onshore winds at the Irish World Cup in 2000, his upwind wave riding was the most remarkable feature of the contest. He was laying the sail down into the trough as he turned off the top, driving the tail so hard into the lip that it literally exploded in a fan of spray.

Front Side Riding

Going 'down the line' (riding downwind facing the wave) is ultimately what it is all about. Bearing away, dropping down the wave and going along it, generates a rush of speed similar to the most sophisticated fairground rides.

Such a thrill comes with a penalty. It is hard enough sailing broad to the wind at full tilt on flat water. Doing the same down the face of a wave is fraught with potential peril. The first time you go front side you are chillingly aware of the fact that the sail is between you and the wave. Should you get it wrong and the wave breaks unexpectedly, you could end up wearing it.

In downwind riding, you also have a bottom and a top turn. The bottom turn, usually long and fast, carries you at speed from the bottom to the top of the wave. The top turn, tighter and 'slashier', redirects the board down the face again.

Effectively, you are doing three-quarters of a gybe – getting to the point of being about to flip the rig and change the feet but then rocking from the toes to the heels on to the upwind edge, sheeting in and carving back the other way.

The bottom turn calls for pure surfing skill. There are infinite variables, depending on the size and speed of the wave and the angle of the wind. The following points, however, apply to all situations.

Speed

Generating speed on the wave face and then carrying it through your bottom turn into every move is essential to fluid, dynamic riding. Without it, the sail gets over-powered and the board sticks into the wave face.

Speed comes from maximizing the slope of the wave. Unless the wave is huge, by dropping vertically down the face you will find yourself out in front and will have lost all your speed by the time it catches up with you. Instead, you should start the ride by angling diagonally down the face. Drop on to the front foot to flat-

ten it off and gun it straight, perhaps doing shallow edge-to-edge 'wiggle' turns to loosen it up. With your speed, you then drop into the bottom turn.

Look!

Observation is everything. As you are lining up and as you drop into the wave, look along it to see where it is walling up and going to break. Rather than bottom turning blindly, look up at the lip and select the spot you want to hit. Look to where you want to be, not at where you are!

Front Foot

To be able to get a board to hold in and turn at more than 40kph (25mph) on the wave face, you have to get the whole edge to engage and grip. The only way to do that is to drop the rig forward, lean down on the boom and commit to the front foot. If this all sounds familiar, gybes and bottom turns share many of the same goals and mistakes – the worst of which is dropping back and turning from the tail.

Observe the world's most powerful wave riders such as Jason Polakow, and the commitment to the turn is breathtak-

The bottom turn is like three-quarters of a hard, fast gybe. The rear hand is right back on the boom to power the sail; you are leaning forward and trying to engage all the rail for maximum speed. Vision is crucial. Look ahead and focus on the section of the wave you want to hit.

Downwind Bottom Turn, Top Turn Sequence *(John Carter)*

The transition to the other edge begins as you start to head back up the wave. Sheet out to avoid being back-winded and let the board come underneath you. (John Carter)

Slide the back hand forward on the boom, open the sail right out in order to push the clew above the wave, turn the head and project everything, shoulders and hips, back down the face. Let the wave hit the underside of the board, redirect it, and help it on its way by driving off the heels. (John Carter)

To gain the perfect 10, sheet in and extend the legs to explode the lip into a fan of spray. See how the whole rail, not just the tail, is biting in the water. (John Carter)

Matt Pritchard is doing about 30kt as he turns at the bottom of this sizeable Hookipa wave. At that speed, the only way he can get the whole edge to bite is to power down through the boom and turn off the front foot. To lean back at this stage is to court certain disaster. Check the head – it should be up and staring at the next section. (John Carter)

ing. They bank the board over so steeply and stretch the rig so far forward that the mast tip sometimes pokes into the wave face. They themselves are so committed that their heads are level with the mast-foot.

Rig Angle

Speed and control through the bottom and top turns come from being ever aware of the wind direction and then keeping the rig powered through the whole sequence. The bottom turn starts like a gybe with the back hand well down the boom in a position to sheet in hard. If the wind is side shore as you turn parallel with the wave, you are already dead downwind and so must immediately open the sail right out. As you climb towards the lip in preparation for your top turn, you are through the wind and unless you keep

opening the sail out into the clew first position, the wind will hit the other side and drill you to the floor. As you turn off the top, slide the back hand forward to avoid over sheeting and close the sail again. It is timing the sheeting in with the leg drive into the edge that gives the top turn its 'snap' and power.

> **TOP TIP**
>
> *Throughout the entire top turn, bottom sequence, you must be constantly moving the back hand and altering the sheeting angle of the sail.*

Top Turn Variations

'Top turn' is the generic name given to any turn done at the top of the wave. Depending on the flamboyance of the interpretation, it may also be described as

a 'cutback', 'off-the-lip' or 'aerial off-the-lip'.

The Cutback

The term 'cutback' is born out of the idea of cutting back towards the 'curl'. On a peeling wave, the bottom turn takes you away from the white water on to the shoulder of the wave. The cutback, more radical than a straight top turn, cranks you right through 180 degrees back to the peak, from where, if the wave is still unwinding, you drop into another sequence.

The Off-The-Lip

The lip is the fastest, most active part of the wave and so to attempt a turn at this point is to guarantee a spectacular result whatever the outcome. As with the back side top turn, the aim is to let the wave do the work.

In a textbook example, you would make a harder, tighter bottom turn and so climb more vertically towards the lip. Sheeted right out, you would present the underside of the board to the pitching lip and let it smack the nose round through 180 degrees. You would then help the redirection by sheeting in and projecting your shoulders and hips down the face.

The Aerial Off-The-Lip

More commonly known just as an 'aerial', this is an off-the-lip where you hit the lip with such speed and timing that it launches you out in front of the wave, from where you land back on the face and carry on. To get your first aerial, it helps to approach the lip from a higher angle. Rather than drop to the bottom and do a hard bottom turn, you stay high on the wave and approach the lip in a faster, shallower arc. The extra speed combined with hitting the lip just as it folds over sends you skywards.

The best time for aerials is in a side offshore wind because that is when you have full power in the sail as you hit the lip.

What it Really Takes

At the beginning of the book, I likened the way you move on the board to dancing. Well, good wave sailors really do dance. They bend like limbo dancers, hurl themselves around like rock 'n rollers or sometimes just sway gently from side to side to the rhythms of Latin America. However, like an inexperienced dancer, in the beginning, although you may know the steps, it is all a bit stilted and you stare at your feet almost oblivious to the needs of your partner. Never forget that the wave is your partner and the more time you spend in its company, the more comfortable you will feel. Gradually, you will develop an instinct as to what it is going to do, you will stop treading on its toes, and go with its energy rather than fighting it.

Away from the dancing analogy, learning to sail in waves is undeniably something of a trial by fire that no amount of reading or studying can prepare you for. Any seasoned campaigner will tell you that the only thing to do is to go out there and get trashed a few hundred times. With every run in and out, you amass a bank of experiences. Every fall and rinsing is logged so next time you will know instinctively not to place yourself in that particular situation again.

A wise surfer once said: 'You can learn to catch the wave and stand up in a couple of days. But as for getting out there and consistently ending up in the right spot to catch the right wave in the right place, that's a lifetime's work.'

After a few sessions, the blinkers start to come off and you will find yourself picking a smarter route through the minefields. As the swim count drops, the pure exhilaration rises. Early progress also has much to do with the choice of training ground. Going out in unsuitable conditions will only teach you that rocks are sharp, boards are fragile and that you should take up something less risky, like BASE jumping. You need to be challenged but not scared witless.

Wave Rules

The best spots can get pretty crowded. At wave sailing headquarters Hookipa beach in Maui, there may be as many as sixty boards all trying to jump and ride the same waves. The potential for collisions and general dispute is huge. However, genuine conflict is quite rare because there are certain clear rules, which are:

1. Riders give way to jumpers. If you are coming in on a wave, you have to keep out of the way of those going out. The reasoning is that you have more speed and more options when riding with the swell.
2. When riding, the sailor nearest the peak has right of way. This is a basic surfing rule. On a wave that is peeling cleanly one way, there is only room for one. But in the likely event that the wave has 'sections' (several spots where it is breaking), then there is room for a few.
3. The first on the wave has right of way. This is really more of a surfing rule where he who gets to his feet first and starts surfing the wave, can claim it. But on a windsurfer you could sail 10 miles out to sea and catch the wave when it

A classic Jason Polakow aerial 'off-the-lip' at Hookipa. An immaculately timed bottom turn has taken him at speed back up to the top of the wave just as it breaks.

Off-the-Lip Sequence *(John Carter)*

He presents the underside of the board to the curling lip, which smacks it and launches him up and out. Anticipating the change of direction, he has already dropped back.

Unbridled flamboyance persuades him to kick the tail out for extra points ...

... before bringing it back into line and landing back on the face. See how everything is projecting towards the new direction. The man is dancing!

has just left home. If anyone quotes this one at you, refer them to rule 2.

4. Watch out! This is not so much a rule as common sense. At a busy spot, there will always be someone taking a swim. In the waves, swimmers are very hard to spot until you are right on top of them. Keep looking around and if you see someone go down, note his position.

Getting your Fair Share

During my first trip to Hawaii, it took me about four days before I caught a wave at Hookipa. This is the most famous and most crowded windsurfing spot in the world, where reputations are made and fragile boards, masts and egos end up shattered on the rocks. I was a young pretender amongst all these legends that I had only ever seen before in magazines and on videos. I spent my whole time either trying to keep of their way or apologizing – an approach which bore little fruit in terms of improving my own skills.

On a busy day in good conditions, you have to fight for your waves – not with bare knuckles but you do have to stand up for your rights. If others sense a little weakness or timidity, they will 'drop in' on you (steal your wave). If you are on the peak, just go for it. They will soon get out of your way and respect you for it.

Wave Sailing Ethos

Let us finish on a high note. Although the upper echelons are dominated by a troupe of young bucks all battling to take it to the next level, the culture of wave sailing is absolutely not about rules, crowds and conflict. Almost everyone does it to escape the masses and hook up with like-minded folk also in search of – and I know this sounds corny – the perfect wave. Also, it is an ideal excuse to travel the world. Australia, New Zealand, the Caribbean Islands, Mexico and Peru are just some of the many countries that boast outstanding, sparsely populated wave sailing spots that demand to be visited.

The fundamental rule in breaking waves is that the sailor going out has right of way over the one coming in riding the wave. (Dave White)

CHAPTER 12

FREESTYLE

My windsurfing career just a few weeks old, I was gliding gently across the beige waters of a gravel pit in Staines just outside London, flattered but slightly surprised at just how many people had lined the banks to watch this steady but seemingly unspectacular performance. My chest soon deflated when I looked over my shoulder to see a board shoot past with the sailor inside the boom on the wrong side of the sail. He tacked round, pirouetting through 360 degrees as he did so before flipping the board up on its side and standing on the edge. It was only a 3–6kt (force 2) wind, he was on the same type of board as me, the original Windsurfer design, but there the comparison ended. It turned out to be the first UK freestyle champion Dee Caldwell honing his routine for the forthcoming world championships, hence the crowd.

Freestyle on the original long boards was watery ballet. There were no fixed rules, you just let your imagination run riot and set about sailing and turning the board in the most bizarre ways possible – sitting down, lying down, standing on your head and so on. In competition, the aim was to link these moves into a flowing three-minute routine. For a while it was considered to be the most illustrious competitive discipline and the standard was amazing. The women, like the USA's Rhonda Smith were wonderfully athletic and supple, performing stunts like a full split on the rail of the board.

The spirit of freestyle is about having a laugh on the water rather than grim-faced athleticism. (John Carter)

Light wind, long-board freestyle remains popular and does wonders for your general sailing. Here, the author (wearing worryingly short shorts) is performing a leeward side 'rail-ride' in the early nineties. (John Carter)

As shorter, high-wind boards flooded the market, freestyle, as a competitive discipline, got put on the back burner. It remained something to do when the wind was light but the attention of the masses turned to planing, speed, carve gybes and a few nifty variations. Then came the revolution.

In 1996, a very low-key event took place on Lake Garda in Italy. Called 'King of the Lake', it was the first short-board freestyle competition. The players had to perform their routine of mostly planing tricks in a square area right next to the shore before a grandstand of manic spectators. There was music, laughter, heavy drinking and non-stop partying. Windsurfing had found a totally new energy.

No one took it too seriously at first but Hawaii-based wave sailors such as Josh Stone and Robbie Seegar set about inventing a whole new style of trickery, loosely labelled 'new school'. The moves were unlike anything ever seen before and

came with eccentric names like Vulcan and Spock. The style, the language, the fashion, the moves themselves and the general spirit borrowed much from snowboarding and skateboarding.

By 1998, it had become a new professional discipline and its arrival was applauded in every quarter (almost). It carried the immediate excitement and spectator appeal of a wave contest but events could be staged anywhere, from the lakes of Austria to the Pacific Ocean. Most importantly of all it brought in a new crop of young sailors, who would never have had the funds to support a racing programme but could afford the one board and three sails you needed to practise and compete at freestyle.

FREESTYLE AND THE COMMON MAN

If you sail along and take one hand off the boom, you are doing freestyle. There are moves ranging from the childishly simple to the unapproachable and unpronounceable. You just find your level. And why indulge in such frippery? Windsurfing is about movement and power control. In freestyle you have to move with speed and precision and handle the rig from all kinds of strange angles. Your general sailing improves beyond all measure. Always having a new trick to go for keeps you motivated and finding new ways to fall off provides much amusement to you and those watching.

OLD SCHOOL VERSUS NEW SCHOOL

This has nothing to do with the age of the rider but more the style of the trick. With a few exceptions, old-school moves are variations on carving tacks and gybes – as a result they can be performed on just about any type of board. New-school moves, on the other hand, often start with a jump or hop. The feet tend to stay in the straps throughout the move and there is usually a sliding element, where the board skids backwards or spins on the nose. Like 'twin tip' snow skis and snowboards that slide either way, the modern freestyle

board is almost as happy going backwards as forwards. Most new-school tricks are difficult without the new style of board.

FREESTYLE EQUIPMENT

A dedicated freestyle board is about 90–115ltr, short and relatively wide throughout. The wide tail helps you pop jumps on flat water. The wide nose has channels under it to help you plane backwards. A crucial accessory is the fin, which is wide for resistance but very short. The shorter the fin, the easier it is to get out of the water if you want to skid the board round in a sort of deliberate spin-out, and the closer you can get to the beach to do your tricks.

People getting on a freestyle board for the first time suddenly find themselves able to do tricks that have confounded them for years. The short, rounded edges push through the water without catching and help you recover from crazy angles. They also not only plane early but also at slow speeds, meaning they keep going through tricks and allow you to attempt moves at a more comfortable pace.

The disadvantage of that width is that they tend to bounce around in chop, especially when over-powered. Like a wave board, you set them up for manoeuvring with the straps mounted near the centreline. As a result, they can be uncomfortable in a straight line.

FREESTYLING CONDITIONS

The top twenty world freestyle ranking list is crammed with people from the Caribbean islands of Margerita and Bonaire – Tati and Tonky Frans, Diony Guadagnino, Douglas Diaz and Ricardo Campello to name a few. Both spots offer ideal freestyling conditions: flat water and winds of 15–25kt (force 4–6). Flat water makes most tricks infinitely easier, especially ones that involve sliding backwards. Rigs much over 6.5sq m are too big and cumbersome to throw around. When experts are in town, there is no upper wind limit. As the waves roll in, the tricks just become more jump-oriented.

Planing switch foot is an integral part of many new and old school tricks. Lean forward and twist at the hips. (John Carter)

Nik Baker controlling the sail from the 'wrong' side at the start of a flaka. (John Carter)

KEY FREESTYLING SKILLS

Without the following four basic freestyling skills, only the simplest tricks are open to you. Each can be practised in isolation and, once you have mastered them, a raft of moves falls within your grasp.

Sailing Clew-First

Sailing with the sail reversed is key to certain gybes (see page 100). The next step is to plane holding the sail clew-first. The tips are to make sure you are well powered up and head off on a very broad reach.

Sailing Switch Foot

'Switch foot' means sailing with your feet in the opposite set of straps or just facing the wrong way. The best way to practise is to carve gybe, release the rig, power up on the new tack and see if you can sail away without moving your feet. The trick is to twist at the hips in order to face the sail and lean forward on to the boom to stop the board heading up.

Sailing Back-Winded

Sailing 'back-winded' means controlling the rig from the wrong side of the sail. You face the wind and resist the force by pushing not pulling. This is one to practise in light winds. It will feel very strange at first since all the controls are reversed. To depower the sail, for example, you pull in the

back hand. As the wind increases there are two essential pointers.

1. Angle the rig right down to windward to decrease the area exposed to the wind. If you get the angle right, the rig balances itself.
2. Never put yourself between the sail and the ocean. If you stand slightly forward of the sail, you can open it and keep out of the way if it gets overpowered.

Chop Hopping

Getting the fin out of the water is the start of many moves. As long as you are on the plane, you should be able to manage it by pumping the sail and driving the power into the back foot. Then, as the board corks back up, stand up and retract the legs to pull the tail clear, at the same time lifting up on the boom. Flat-water hops get exponentially more difficult the bigger the board and sail you use and the lighter the wind.

AN ENDLESS QUEST

If ever there was a way,to age a book it would be to talk about the latest freestyle tricks. New tricks are like computers – there is always something new. Freestyle is such a fertile breeding ground that not even the top judges can keep up with everything. 'What the hell was that?' is a common cry in the judges' booth. At the

last count there were well over one hundred recognized tricks, far too many to cover in one chapter. Here, however, is a brief description of the classic old and new-school moves.

Old-School Tricks

No specialist equipment is needed. So long as your board planes and carves a turn, you can have a go at all the classics.

One-Handed Gybes
As the back hand releases during the carve gybe or the duck gybe, it reaches down and strokes the water to the inside of the turn on its way to the new side of the boom.

> **TOP TIP**
> *Reach forward with the hand so you stroke the water level with the front foot.*

The Carving 360
This carve gybe where you don't stop turning could be described as the original functionless manoeuvre – a lot of spray and effort to end up heading in the same direction.

You bank the board over at the time you normally flip the rig, hang on and lay it right down to the inside and sweep it back over the tail. The wind fills from the other side and drives the tail round. As you

The carving 360 is the king of the old-school tricks. You bank the board as if into a super-tight radius gybe and lay the rig right down to the floor.

Wind
Direction

At the moment that you would normally flip the rig, the wind hits it from the other side and you sweep it right back over the tail.

Carving 360 Sequence *(Dave White)*

Head to wind, you throw the rig forward again and sheet in to bear away and complete the spin. This more advanced version was done in the straps all the way round. It is easier to step forward half-way through to keep the board level as it slows down.

come round head to wind, you sheet in to catch the wind from the original side and bear away to complete the rotation.

With speed and practice, you can do the whole manoeuvre in the straps. When learning, however, it helps to step the front foot up to the mastfoot as the board slows down.

TOP TIP
Never let the pressure off the inside edge and never look back at the tail when the sail back-winds.

The Body Drag
Innocent bystanders marvel at this classic yet readily achievable piece of showmanship, where, on the plane, you throw yourself into the water and 'drag' alongside the board before letting the rig pull you back on.

Planing across the wind, head up on to a close reach, then step both legs off the board to windward as far away from the edge as you can. Pull yourself right up to the boom, keep the rig upright, and aim to plane just on the tops of your thighs and

shins ('leg drag' would be a better title). Lever down on the boom to bear the nose away. The increase in power should be enough to pull you back up.

TOP TIP
Bend the arms and keep your torso clear of the water.

The body drag is another classic. Step away from the board, keep the rig upright and drag just on the tops of your legs. (John Carter)

Monkey Gybes

For some reason beloved by the Germans, the monkey gybe and its variations involve a sail and body 360 in the middle of the gybe as part of the rig change. It can be done in the middle of either a duck or a carve gybe.

> **TOP TIP**
>
> *Keep the speed up. The faster you go downwind, the lighter the rig is and the easier the spin.*

The Helicopter Tack

Pretty straightforward in light winds on a big board, this upwind turn takes on another life in planing winds on a small board.

Steer into wind as if you were doing a normal tack, but instead of walking around the mast, push the rig down to windward and forward to back-wind the sail. Bear away by easing the rig towards the nose. Now comes the 'helicopter' bit. Lean the rig right towards the nose, push the clew through the wind and as the rig spins round, follow it round with the feet. Either

release the rig immediately or come out clew-first. Controlling the rig back-winded is the key skill.

> **TOP TIP**
>
> *You have to switch your feet round as quickly as you can and get them in position on the centreline before the rig swings round.*

The Duck Tack

This will earn you deep respect from your peers. In a switch-foot stance, carve into wind and with a rig action similar to the duck gybe, throw the sail directly into the wind and 'duck' under the foot of the sail to reach the new side.

> **TOP TIP**
>
> *The faster you carve into wind, the easier it is.*

New-School Tricks

Be prepared to leap, spin, slide and twist – this is skateboarding taken to the water. Most of the following are not for those

with weak ankles, unstable knees or dodgy backs.

The Vulcan

Arguably the original new-school trick, this is an aerial gybe where you pop a jump, twist the board through 180 degrees, flip the rig in mid-air, land sailing backwards on the nose, power up on the new tack and change the feet.

> **TOP TIP**
>
> *Bear away before jumping so you have less far to turn, and land leaning forward on the front foot. That way the tail stays high and you will slide back without it catching.*

The Spock

Perhaps the most classic of all the new tricks, the Spock is a Vulcan that just keeps going for another 180 degrees.

Get to the point where you are sliding backwards on the nose; but instead of sheeting in and going back the other way, lean forward on to the boom to back the sail and keep the board spinning round on the nose. As it comes round, let the rig swing round over the nose. There is also a Spock 540 where you keep it spinning round another 180 degrees but words are all too impotent a medium to describe its complexity.

> **TOP TIP**
>
> *As the board spins round, hold the rig as far forward towards the nose as you can.*

The Willy Skipper

This is one of the few new moves where the feet come out of the straps. It is also appreciably easier than most.

Planing across the wind, take the back foot out of the strap. Then pop the board out of the water, kick away with the front leg and pull in with the back leg to spin the board through 180 degrees in the air. Stay sheeted in and aim to land sailing backwards with the front foot right up by the mastfoot. There are many ways to end this move, the easiest is to slide to a stop, move the hands to the other side of the

'Irie Man' Brian Talma from Barbados finishing off a Vulcan. He has just jumped the board around and flipped the sail in mid-air. He's now sliding backwards on the nose before sheeting in and heading off forward again. (John Carter)

boom and head off in the opposite direction.

The Upwind 360

This is a delightful trick in that it is not only readily achievable by mortal man but also has a simple grace and fluidity.

It starts like a helicopter tack. Turn into wind and back the sail. Use it to bear you right away until you are almost downwind. Push the clew through the wind and as the sail fills from the other side, the sudden pressure whips you round to complete the 360. In its end form in planing winds, the feet stay in the straps all the way round.

LEARNING A NEW TRICK

There are so many more tricks – flakas, takas, grubbies, cha chas, monkey flips – the list goes on and on, and most of them can be done switch-foot or clew-first for extra points. Getting your head around the names is one thing but how do you go about performing them?

Some people, especially men, are their own worst enemies when it comes to learning a new move. They tend to try it time and time again, hoping that it will just suddenly come right. And so it might – however, unless you have some sort of strategy, the chances are pretty remote. This is how you might approach a new challenge.

Preparation

First, you must have a clear idea of what the trick involves. Become well acquainted with what happens at every stage by looking at a video, reading a book or magazine, talking to an expert or watching it for real. Then sit down and try to imagine yourself doing it. Mental rehearsal or 'visualization' is an essential preparation tool used by all top sportsmen.

Next, you should ask yourself whether this is a move you have to approach in one hit, or would it be possible to break it down and practise it in sections? In the monkey gybe, for example, you can work on sail and body 360s off the plane and then try them on the plane before feeding one into the gybe itself.

Feedback and Observation

Cracking a complicated move is all about training your memory. In the beginning there is no substitute for just giving it a go in order to get a general feel for what's going on. But remember, your body does not differentiate between good and bad technique, it just knows the path most trodden, which is why mistakes quickly become habit forming.

If, after half a dozen attempts, you are none the wiser, get off the water and seek help. Useful feedback may come either from a training partner or from video, the supreme learning aid. As the camera cannot lie, it forces you to relate the perception you have of yourself to the reality, which can be quite scary.

Good sailors are also good watchers. As you try to get a deeper insight into the manoeuvre, look at quite specific things like the angle to the wind on take-off, the position of the body relative to the board, and, if there are any, the timing of any rig and foot changes.

Take a Break

Repeated failure can quickly turn enthusiasm into frustration. The more you fail, the more your head fills with analytical rubbish and the more you tighten up. Before the water turns blue and you start attacking

John Hibbard about to flip the sail around his back to finish off a Spock. (John Carter)

Ladies' champion Karin Jaggi performing a Willy-Skipper. She has flipped the board around in mid-air and is about to land planing backwards with her feet out of the straps. (John Carter)

your equipment, go off for a sail and have a bit of fun. Many of the top performers have what they call a 'trigger' move, which is a trick or just a simple manoeuvre that they know they can do really well every time. By doing it, the body frees up, starts moving naturally and is ready to try again.

The Right Moment
Choose your moment carefully. Different tricks favour different conditions. It is fruitless to go for a carving 360 if you are barely planing. Likewise, a helicopter tack is especially difficult if you have been hit by a huge gust. In general, for downwind carving and aerial tricks it helps to be fully powered, whilst for upwind tricks like the helicopter tack, duck tack and the upwind 360, it helps to be slightly underpowered.

Keep your Form
As you try to get mind and body around a new set of moves, it is all too easy to forget the basics of balance and form, and return to that robotic, stiff beginner state.

With all new tricks, it is essential to remember to keep your weight centred. Whether you are doing a Vulcan or a simple tack, you have the greatest chance of saving the move if you keep your centre of gravity over the middle of the board.

It is equally important to find the 'key' to a trick. You can get close just by watching and practising, but for every trick there is often a nugget of advice, a precious key that suddenly unlocks it for you. Here are three gems of wisdom that have worked for me.

1. Looking at your feet when you do a spin or pirouette (in the monkey gybe for example) somehow keeps you orientated.
2. In the duck gybe, look under the foot of the sail to the new side of the boom.
3. In the duck tack, bear away a little before you switch your feet and carve upwind. The extra speed makes the board more stable as you first take up the switch stance.

CHAPTER 13

WINDSURFING COMPETITION

As a way to get rid of stress, windsurfing has no equal. There is so much going on around you that the brain has no time to mull over problems. Hence you emerge physically exhausted but mentally refreshed. So why would you want to turn it into a battle, get all those combative chemicals coursing back through your veins and generally work yourself up into a lather? Well, the fact that 90 per cent of windsurfers never go anywhere near a contest area and do it entirely for fun tells its own story.

However, if I may put the case for the defence, competitive windsurfing is thrilling, uplifting and played out by mostly fun-loving, well-balanced people. The regional and national events are more akin to festivals. Hundreds of like-minded folk are brought together by a mutual love of the sport, the atmosphere is fantastic, and the friendships formed, lifelong.

That same camaraderie pervades the highest levels. With the world speed championships at stake, I broke a mast during the last hour of competition. My greatest rival left the water and ran back to the rigging tent to get me his spare one (he actually went on to beat me). There are many such stories. Happily, and yet

Professional windsurfing has huge spectator appeal. Crowds pack the grandstand for the PWA freestyle championships at Sotavento in Fuerteventura. (John Carter)

The advantage of traditional, long raceboards is that racing can take place in as little as 5kt. An Olympic qualifying fleet in action. The letters on the sail denote the nationality of the competitor.

somehow sadly, the financial rewards are insufficient to turn the stars into lofty, Ferrari-driving prima donnas.

Competition is the sport's showcase and is largely responsible for the continual improvements in equipment. Designs and materials developed out on the racetrack inevitably filter down into recreational models.

On a personal level, the greatest by-product of a competition is how it immediately improves your skill and technique. Every aspect of your game is tested – wind awareness, tuning, fitness and of course your technique.

There are a number of competitive disciplines but they can loosely be divided into racing and judged events such as freestyle and wave sailing.

THE OLYMPICS

Windsurfing first became an Olympic sport at the Los Angeles games of 1984. Like the other yachting classes, the event is a 'one-class design' – in other words, the boards being used are identical in every respect. A series of races takes place around a course with upwind, downwind and reaching legs.

Right from the earliest days, Olympic windsurfing grew apart from mainstream windsurfing and has never really represented the pinnacle of achievement in the eyes of the public. Indeed the first Olympic champion, Stefan van den Berg of The Netherlands, although famous in his own country, received less international recognition than that year's professional

champion Robby Naish. The reasons are many. Light-wind course racing is visually less exciting than the high-wind, high-action disciplines. With the Olympics often being staged at light-wind venues and with everyone being forced to use the same size sail, you have very little chance of success if you weigh much over 70kg (155lb). Only one woman and one man can qualify from each country. The Olympic board itself is a very old design and much less exciting to sail than the latest planing hulls.

Nonetheless, our Olympic windsurfers are incredibly fit and skilful. To generate extra speed, they pump their rigs for the duration of the race – the equivalent of doing about 2,000 chin-ups – while making tactical decisions at the same time.

However, the future looks bright. There are moves afoot to bring in a more modern board design for the Beijing games in 2008.

The Olympic board is raced recreationally all over the world in the raceboard class. It remains popular, especially on sheltered inland waters, because racing can take place in the lightest winds.

FORMULA RACING

Formula is a restricted open class, meaning you can use any make of board or rig but they have to fall within certain measurements. For example, the fin must not be longer than 70cm (27in) and the board not wider than 1m (3ft). To prevent it becoming a war of cheque books, you are limited to one board and four rigs, which have to be registered at the beginning of the season.

The format, the basic rules and the courses are much the same as for Olympic racing. The main difference is that because there is a minimum wind speed of 8kt and the sailors use rigs as big as 12sq m, these races take place at speed on the plane.

In course racing you may be sharing the start line with sixty boards or more. Your one aim is to hit that line at full speed as the gun goes. If you get away well, you will find yourself in clear wind and in position to dictate the race. If you are caught in the second row, you will flounder in the wind shadow of other boards and have limited tactical options. So start in front and stay in front!

The Formula course is fundamentally a series of upwind and downwind legs. To excel on both you have to be massively powered and hence take out the biggest sail possible. It is very physical but there is so much more to it than that. The best sailors are acutely aware of their surroundings and plot their course according to the tide, the wind shifts and the movements of their nearest rivals. They are totally in tune with their equipment. Ropes running to cleats on either side of the boom allow them to adjust the profile of the sail as they go along for different points of sailing.

A Formula fleet flying up the beat. Success comes from a mixture of speed and tactics. (John Carter)

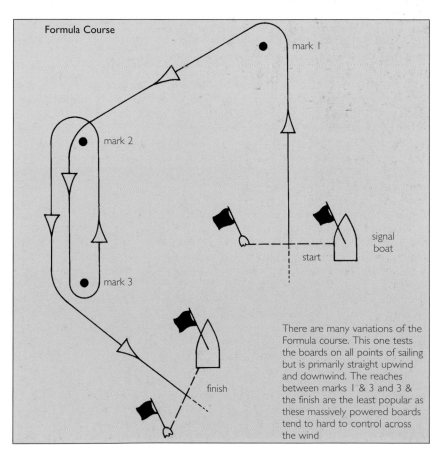

Formula Course

mark 1

mark 2

mark 3

start

signal boat

finish

There are many variations of the Formula course. This one tests the boards on all points of sailing but is primarily straight upwind and downwind. The reaches between marks 1 & 3 and 3 & the finish are the least popular as these massively powered boards tend to hard to control across the wind

SLALOM

Slalom is arguably the most thrilling of all the racing formats. It runs on a knockout system. Heats of between ten and twenty sailors race across the wind around a figure of eight or similar course with the top half of the fleet going through to the next round.

Whereas course racing is primarily about tactics, slalom is the ultimate test of speed and board handling. One of my most memorable races was at Tarifa in southern Spain in wind speeds of 34–40kt (a solid force 8). The first leg sent the ten of us 500m (550yd) down the speed course. We were doing more than 64kph (40mph) as we all banked into the first gybe mark, all trying to bag the inside slot. The potential for carnage was greater than at the first corner of a Grand Prix.

Sometimes the courses are laid within the surf line. The sight of the whole fleet hitting a wave and getting simultaneously airborne is something to behold. When sea conditions are severe, the sailors often start from the beach, run into the sea and launch 'Le Mans style'.

The attraction of slalom is its simplicity. All recreational boards are designed to plane across the wind and gybe so there is no need for specialist kit. As the courses are easy to set up, you will probably find a number of spontaneous local events.

SUPER X

At a professional level, slalom was criticized for being too processional. Once somebody takes the lead, it is very hard to overtake unless he falls. Consequently, it was all becoming a bit predictable, especially when you had the likes of twelve-times world champion Bjorn Dunkerbeck hogging the front spot. However, Super X, the latest professional discipline, provokes endless mishaps and lead changing by adding compulsory jumping and freestyle elements.

After a running start you follow a downwind course. However, on some of the legs you will find floating hurdles, which you have to jump over; down other legs, you have to perform certain freestyle tricks. With full body contact guaranteed, racers wear motocross-style helmets and body armour in what has become a 'made for TV' spectacular.

SPEED SAILING

Speed events are a simple challenge as to who can go the fastest over a set distance – a race against the clock. You are timed between two transits and the average speed is calculated. To count as an official record, the course has to be 500m (550yd) long but regional events can be run over shorter courses of 100m (110yd).

Speed sailing as a professional discipline was overtaken in popularity by freestyle but has recently made a resurgence. Frenchman Thierry Bielak's speed record of 45.5kt stood for ten years until December 2003 when it was taken to 46.24kt by Finian Maynard of the Virgin Islands. It is a phenomenal speed, but given the advances in equipment, many believe that it is possible not only to beat the overall sailing speed record of 46.6kt set by the specialist catamaran 'Yellow Pages' but also to break the 50kt barrier. All the recent windsurfing records have been set on the famous 'Canal de Vitesse'. It is a 1km long, man-made trench cut into the beach of Les Saintes Maries de la Mer in the south of France. Irreverently referred to as the 'Speed Ditch' by jealous Brits, it provides silky smooth water and lies at the perfect direction to the brutal Mistral wind.

To drive a windsurfer to that sort of speed takes storm force winds blowing at about a 140-degree angle to glassy, flat water. You need highly specialized kit. Speed boards, otherwise known as 'guns' or 'needles' are as narrow as 35cm (14in) and look more like water-skis. The rigs

The fleet gathers by the start boat so they can set their watches as the red preparatory flag is raised.

Four Stages of a Slalom Race *(John Carter)*

If they have timed their run right, they cross the line at full speed exactly when the gun goes.

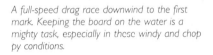
A full-speed drag race downwind to the first mark. Keeping the board on the water is a mighty task, especially in these windy and choppy conditions.

Now for the tricky bit – negotiating the gybe mark at full planing speed, trying to take the best line in order to overtake or close the door on your rivals.

have to handle perhaps twice the amount of power as a normal sail and are wing-like in their stability. The driver has to be strong, skilful and brave to the point of stupidity as there are serious consequences from slamming into the water at 80kph (50mph).

As the chances of all the right elements coming together at the same spot on an allotted day are very slim, it has become a waiting game. Well-prepared teams hang out at the best spots for months on end waiting for that elusive combination of flat water and a perfectly angled hurricane.

Traditionally, this is a big man's game. The heavier you are, the bigger the sail you can hold down and the more power you can drive into the board. Those lacking natural kilos take to wearing weight jackets, which are as uncomfortable and as bad for your back as they sound. There is more than a little truth in the maxim 'fat is fast' but the ability to keep the board and sail trimmed in the craziest winds is far more important than mere ballast.

Speed sailing at a recreational level will always be popular. Everyone wants to go faster than their friends and the best part of all is that you can enter competitions without being able to gybe!

JUNIOR RACING AND TEAM 15

There has never been a better time to be a young windsurfer. The initiative 'Team 15' gets children up to the age of fifteen into competitive windsurfing in the cheapest and easiest way possible. There are over seventy-five Team 15 clubs around the country. At some the children bring their own boards, at others they are provided. The format is chosen to suit the people and the conditions. It might be a straight 'there and back' race, a figure of eight slalom or a course race.

From here, a choice of pathways opens up. If the youngsters aspire to compete in the Olympics, they can join the various RYA training squads. If they are moving towards Formula or waves and freestyle, they should join the UKWA (United Kingdom Windsurfing Association) who run those disciplines (see page 174).

WAVE COMPETITIONS

Wave competitions are judged in heats, generally of four sailors, who perform before a panel of judges after which the most impressive two or three advance to the next round. How exactly the event is scored will depend on the conditions. Sometimes jumping scores more highly, other times they may only be judged on riding. On a day with a good side-shore wind, which is good for both, a heat will usually last ten minutes. During this time, they will be scored on their best three jumps and best three wave rides.

Like gymnastics, each move has a tariff. A back loop, for example, scores more than a forward loop. A double forward loop scores higher than a back loop but a double back loop (yet to be landed in competition) scores highest of all. The sailors get marked up for variety and marked down for repetition. In wave riding, they are scored on their choice of wave and then what they do on it. Judges like to see them staying within the critical section right where it's breaking and using the wave to generate their speed and power. True aerials, where, thanks to exquisite timing, the curling lip launches the board skywards, score especially highly.

Wave contests are very tactical. The veterans, while no longer the most spectacular performers, so often beat the younger opposition just by being smart. They are very good at staying upwind and doing their stuff right in front of the judges. They make sure they put in the required jumps and rides early. Then in the last couple of minutes of the heat, they go for the big moves. They also play an astute psychological game. Often, as the flag is raised at the start of the heat, they will do a clean move right in front of their rival to leave him playing a game of catch-up.

Less experienced, though naturally talented sailors sometimes lose track of where they are. After a couple of rides, they find themselves downwind, out of the contest area. Ruled by their exuberance, they often panic, go for an unnecessarily huge move in the first minute and end up taking a swim and wasting precious time

Bjorn Dunkerbeck, using a very narrow speed board and a specially designed double skin rig, is determined to reclaim the overall sailing speed record and be the first to reach 50kt. (John Carter)

and energy. Although it appears to be the preserve of the young and supple, experience counts for a lot. The legendary Robby Naish was sweeping aside pubescent pretenders way into his late thirties.

FREESTYLE

The judging format is very much the same as for waves. It is a knockout format where heats, again generally of four, perform in a defined area in front of a panel. The difference is that they are marked simply on overall impression. Difficulty of tricks, originality, style, and how the moves are linked into a fluid routine are the elements that are taken into account.

The meteoric rise in the general standard has made life almost impossible for judges. The tricks are so quick and complex and they follow each other so quickly that the results between the top players are becoming ever harder to call. Computerized score pads are the suggested way forward.

Freestyle contests are held in all conditions, from the moderate wind and flat water of Bonaire to the gales and chop of Gran Canaria and Fuerteventura. When freestyle moves into the waves and the tricks become more jump-oriented, it also goes under the name of 'free move'.

Freestyle competition at lower levels is popular because it can be run in just about any wind strength. In non-planing winds, competitors just have to take out a bigger board and perform a more old-school routine of sail and board spins and pirouettes.

INDOOR WINDSURFING

Many thought it was an April Fool joke when a magazine announced that the first indoor windsurfing event was to be staged in the Bercy stadium in Paris. This outrageous concept, the brainchild of Fred Beauchene, the first man to windsurf the Atlantic, was massively popular throughout the nineties with events springing up in cities such as Barcelona, Vienna and Istanbul. A purpose-built pool is erected and a bank of industrial fans provides a wind of 30kt (force 7).

The chosen disciplines are slalom, waves and freestyle. In slalom, the boards slide into the pool via specially designed ramps and complete three or four laps of a tight figure of eight course. It is one of the most exhausting events imaginable. The wind is brutally gusty and you have no chance to settle into the harness before you are into the next gybe.

For the jumps, competitors fly off a floating ramp and are marked on height, style and smoothness of landing. Frenchmen Eric Thieme and Robert Teritehau from New Caledonia were famous for attacking it with such vigour that they flew out of the pool altogether. They lived to tell the tale! The true star of indoor windsurfing is England's Nik Baker who won the overall championships no less than five times.

Due to the exorbitant cost of staging such an event, the indoor tour died out towards the end of the millennium but has since been resurrected by the organizers of the London Boat Show. The latest event takes place in London's docklands in January.

To get the best conditions, the exact site for wave sailing contests is often decided on the day. This mobile race headquarters for the world cup event in Ireland was pulled on to the beach by a tractor. (John Carter)

GLOSSARY

Aerial Prefix signifying that the move is completed off the water, for example 'aerial gybe'.

Apparent Wind The combination of the true wind and the head wind created by the windsurfer moving forward through the air.

Back-Wind To invite the wind to hit the 'wrong' side of the sail by pushing on the boom. Sailing back-winded means controlling the sail from the downwind side facing the wind.

Bear Away To alter course downwind

Beating Sailing a zig-zag course, either upwind or downwind.

Carve To bank the board over so it 'carves' around on its inside edge.

Centreline The imaginary line running nose to tail down the middle of the board.

Clew The bottom corner of the sail away from the mast.

Daggerboard The retractable keel that fits through the middle of the board. Only fitted on big boards.

Deck-Plate The device that screws into the mast-track and which accommodates the mastfoot assembly.

Downhaul A rope that attaches the bottom of the sail to the mastfoot.

Downwind Direction to which the wind is blowing.

Dump The act of a wave peaking up and crashing heavily.

Foot The bottom edge of the sail.

Freestyle Mostly non-functional, flamboyant moves – performed for the sheer hell of it!

Gybe A downwind turn where the back of the board passes through the eye of the wind.

Head Up To alter course towards the wind.

Knot One nautical mile per hour. One nautical mile (approx. 2,000yd) denotes one minute of latitude.

Leeward Downwind.

Lip The crest of the wave as it is pitching over.

Luff The leading edge of the sail.

Marginal Describes a wind that is almost, but not quite, strong enough to make you plane.

Mastfoot The device at the bottom of the mast that connects the rig to the board.

Mast-track The recess on the deck of the board that accommodates the deck-plate and mastfoot.

Nose The front section of the board.

One Design A class of racing boards of identical design, such as the Olympic Class.

Outhaul A rope that attaches the clew to the end of the boom.

Plan Shape The outline of the board as viewed from above.

Plane To skim like a speedboat across the top of the water rather than plough through it.

Port The left-hand side when facing the front of the board. Traditionally indicated by the colour red.

Pump To move the sail in and out in such as a way to increase the airflow and therefore the power.

Rail *n*. The edge of the board. *vb* A longboard technique for sailing upwind, where you allow the daggerboard to lift the windward edge.

Rig *n*. The combination of mast, sail, boom and mastfoot. *vb* The act of piecing it all together.

Rocker The curve through the board as viewed from the side.

Sheet In Pull the sail in so as to lessen the angle between the board and the foot of the sail.

Sheet Out Open the sail and increase the angle between the board and the foot of the sail.

Shorebreak The heavy waves that break right at the water's edge.

Spin-Out The act of the fin suddenly losing its grip to leave the board sliding sideways.

Spreader Bar The bar across the front of the harness to which the hook is attached, designed to divert the load away from the hips and onto the back.

Starboard The right-hand side when facing the front of the board, traditionally indicated by the colour green.

Tack An upwind turn where the nose of the board passes through the eye of the wind; also the describes the bottom corner of the sail by the mastfoot.

Tacking Upwind/Downwind see Beating

Universal Joint (UJ) The rubber or plastic joint at the bottom of the mastfoot, which allows the rig to fall in every direction.

Waterstart The means of getting going where the rig lifts you up onto the board.

Windward Upwind: for example, the windward side of the board is the side the wind hits first.

USEFUL ADDRESSES

Royal Yachting Association
RYA House
Ensign Way
Hamble
Southampton
SO31 4YA

Tel: +44 (0) 845 345 0400

www.rya.org.uk
www.team15.org.uk

Whereabouts of all registered schools (UK and abroad)
Instructor training
Junior and senior competition
Training videos/DVDs
Olympic Windsurfing
All general windsurfing matters

ISAF (International Sailing Federation)
Ariadne House
Town Quay
Southampton
Hampshire
SO14 2AQ

Tel: +44 (0) 23 80 635111
Fax: +44 (0) 23 80 635789

e-mail: secretariat@isaf.co.uk
www.sailing.org

Addresses of all the International sailing/windsurfing bodies

United Kingdom Windsurfing Association UKWA
12 Beach Court
Old Fort Road
Shoreham Beach
West Sussex
BN43 5RG

Tel: +44 (0)1273 454654
Fax: +44 (0) 1273 454630

e-mail: info@ukwindsurfing.com
www.ukwindsurfing.com

UK Competition Scene – Formula, wave-sailing and Freestyle

Windsurf magazine
Blue Barns
Tew Lane
Wootton
Woodstock
Oxon
OX20 1HA

Tel: +44 (0) 1993 811181

e-mail: info@windsurf.co.uk

Boards magazine
196 Eastern Esplanade
Southend on Sea
Essex
SS1 3AB

Tel: +44 (0) 1702 588434

e-mail: info@boards.co.uk

Professional Windsurfers Association (PWA)
PO Box 791656
Paia
HI 96779
USA

www.pwaworldtour.com

The international professional scene. Race reports, profiles of the stars, event calendar.

INDEX